Bernard Moses

The Federal Government of Switzerland

Bernard Moses

The Federal Government of Switzerland

ISBN/EAN: 9783337157593

Printed in Europe, USA, Canada, Australia, Japan

Cover: Foto ©ninafisch / pixelio.de

More available books at **www.hansebooks.com**

THE

FEDERAL GOVERNMENT

OF

SWITZERLAND

AN ESSAY ON THE CONSTITUTION

BY

BERNARD MOSES, Ph. D.

PROFESSOR OF HISTORY AND POLITICAL ECONOMY,
UNIVERSITY OF CALIFORNIA

OAKLAND, CALIFORNIA:
PACIFIC PRESS PUBLISHING CO.,
SAN FRANCISCO: 18 POST STREET.   NEW YORK: 43 BOND STREET,
LONDON: 48 PATERNOSTER ROW.
1889

CONTENTS.

CHAP.		PAGE.
I.	INTRODUCTORY	1
II.	ANTECEDENTS OF SWISS FEDERALISM	10
III.	THE DISTRIBUTION OF POWER	56
IV.	THE LEGISLATURE	97
V.	THE EXECUTIVE	121
VI.	THE JUDICIARY	140
VII.	FOREIGN RELATIONS	164
VIII.	INTERNAL RELATIONS	178
IX.	THE ARMY AND THE FINANCES	189
X.	RIGHTS AND PRIVILEGES	203
XI.	THE COMMON PROSPERITY	226

CHAPTER I.

INTRODUCTORY.

THE territory of Switzerland is not wholly included within any natural boundaries. The canton of Schaffhausen lies north of the Rhine; on the east Graubünden is separated from Tyrol and Italy only by an arbitrary line; on the south Ticino extends beyond the Alps; and on the west there is no natural boundary coinciding with the political boundary. It is a land of marked peculiarities, the most conspicuous of which are its elevation, its broken surface, and its abundant water. Its elevation ranges from 646 feet at Lake Maggiore, to 15,217 feet on Monte Rosa. Within two degrees of latitude it embraces the climate of thirty-four degrees. It occupies a large part of the summit region of Europe, although Mont Blanc, the highest point of this region, stands without its border. Of the total area of Switzerland, 15,964 square miles, that portion of the surface which has an elevation less than 1,000 feet is about two per cent. of the whole. Between 1,000 and 2,500 feet there is an amount of the surface equal to 37 per cent. of the whole; between 2,500 and 4,000 feet, 21 per cent.; over 4,000 feet, 34 per cent.; while six per cent. of the whole surface is covered with snow-fields and glaciers. By another classification, 11,443 square miles are set down as "productive," and 4,521 square miles as "unproductive." The greater portion of the territory is embraced within two mountain masses, the Jura extending from Geneva to Schaffhausen, and the Alps occupying the southern cantons. The Jura is composed of a number of parallel ridges with intervening valleys. The Alps, on the other hand, are made up of one great ridge supported by far-reaching buttresses. The valleys which lie between these buttresses, particularly those north of the main ridge, are specially the scene of the characteristic life of the Swiss. But the most remarkable feature of this mountain region is its abundant water sources. Within a small district about the St. Gothard, arise important streams, which flow into four distinct seas. The Rhine passes first into Lake Constance, and thence into the North Sea. The Rhone rushes into the Lake of Geneva, which sends it forth purified to the Mediterranean. The Ticino, gathering on the southern slope of the Alps,

INTRODUCTORY 3

joins the Po and is carried on to the Adriatic; while the Inn falls into an eastern valley, and then, in union with the Danube, is lost in the Black Sea. From this point of view Switzerland appears like a great reservoir, whose refreshing waters are sent to the four quarters of Europe.

The population of the territory now under the dominion of the Swiss Republic has undergone fewer changes through migration or foreign interference than that of most lands of Western civilization. It may, therefore, be contrasted with those societies which have grown up in America from English or Spanish settlements. In the one case, there has been growth from pre-historic stock without serious disturbing influences. In the other case, the societies have been formed from elements whose later environment has had little in common with their earlier surroundings, and under conditions where the force of ancient traditions has been weakened by long migration. In the one case, the isolated communities have been crowded together by the external pressure of hostile states. In the other case, the individual settlements have been drawn together by the desire to satisfy their economic wants under more favorable conditions. In the one case, liberty and equality have been fought for in the face of absolutism and aristocratic tendencies. In the other case, particularly in the British settlements, liberty and equality were, in a certain sense, imposed upon the people by the circumstances of colonial life. Yet, however favorable to liberty and equality may have been the conditions of colonial life in some parts of America, there existed in other parts a superior counteracting force in the despotic traditions of the mother country. This was particularly true with reference to the Spanish colonies which were planted in the New World in the sixteenth century. Of these, Mexico is a conspicuous example. Although now in the list of federal republics, yet it could not claim even nominal independence and liberty till after three centuries of uncompromising despotism. Most English colonial dependencies have worked their way to prominence through a struggling age of feebleness, and in the effort have prepared themselves to win and defend their liberty. But the Spanish dependencies have been from the outset equipped with ample legal machinery, and been controlled and supported by the sagacity and power of the monarch, and in this state of complete subordination have lost much of the self-assertion and self-control which are requisite to the character of a free people.

Switzerland and the British colonies in America were predetermined to federation by their geographical positions. Switzerland, particularly that portion of it in which was formed the original union, is composed of valleys separated from one another by mountains so far impassible as to limit to the inhabitants of each valley the development of the community sentiment. The local independence acquired by the several isolated communities made them unwilling for centuries to join any union closer than that involved in an offensive and defensive alliance; and when finally a strictly federal power was created by the adoption of the constitution of 1848, it was done in opposition to the vote of the cantons of Wallis, Thurgau, Appenzell-Interior, Schwyz, Unterwalden, Uri, and Zug. The federal form was realized under the force of external pressure and the need of a common internal administration, but the consolidation of all the cantons into a centralized State was quite out of the question.

In that portion of America which became the territory of the United States, " the long stretch of coast facing Europe, furthered the establishment of a series of settlements independent of one another and only subordinated to a distant power. The considerable independence which the several colonies thus acquired exerted a powerful influence to make the national government a federal government; for they had so long pursued a separate and individual existence that no closer union was immediately possible. The two alternatives which the makers of the Constitution had to face were federation and anarchy."[1]

Of important existing republics, Switzerland alone antedates the Protestant Revolution, and is consequently the only one that has lived through the period in which religious wars were a part of the order of the day. The effect of this revolution in Switzerland, as in Germany and France, was to form a new ground of party differences, and to divide the Confederation into two hostile camps. The policy adopted was essentially that of Germany, according to which each State enforced uniformity of worship. "The rights of conscience were ignored by Catholics and Protestants alike."[2] The old pugnacity of the Swiss came once more to the front, and to them a religion that was worth having appeared worth fighting for. The religious controversies, which arose from the revival of interest in the doctrine of peace and good-will towards men, threatened the unity of the Confederation and filled the land with the uproar of a civil war. The Catholic cantons stood in continued antagonism to the growth of a central power, but ulti-

---

[1] "Data of Mexican and United States History," by the present writer, in "Papers of the California Historical Society," I, p. 17.

[2] May "Democracy in Europe," 1, 382.

mately the patriotic desire for a more complete union prevailed, and a federal government was established under which both Catholics and Protestants live without serious friction.

The conglomerate character of the Swiss population, composed of representatives of the German, French, and Italian peoples, has made it difficult to bring all parts to co-operate towards a common national end. The fact that these representatives of different peoples have continued in separate groups, each within its own territory, and speaking its own language, has made the growth of a national sentiment slower than it might have been had all been thrown together into a common society and compelled in the course of time to use a common language. At present German is spoken in fourteen cantons and parts of others; French wholly in three cantons and in parts of three others, while Italian is confined to the canton of Ticino and a part of Graubünden. To state the relations between these groups in another way, there are 1,352 German communes, 945 French, and 291 Italian. Besides these there are 118 communes in Graubünden where the Romansch language is used. Only German, French, and Italian, however, are regarded as official languages, and in these three all the federal laws are published, and they may all be used in the transaction of federal business, whether in the assemblies, in the council, or in the courts. Moreover, all must be represented in the Federal Council. The Romansch language, on the other hand, is not an official language, and is seldom employed in the affairs of the federal government Not only as it regards their language, but in a general way also as it regards their manners and customs, have the several cantons maintained their individuality.

While in Switzerland the representatives of the German, French, and Italian peoples have preserved their peculiar characteristics, to a certain extent, by remaining territorially separated, in the United States there has been a mingling of peoples on the same territory, and there is already manifest a tendency to mould those of English, Scotch, Irish, German, and Scandinavian stock into a new national product. But in the Southern States of the Union, the presence of the negro introduces a problem, of which the population of Switzerland gives no hint.

The recognition of members of different races as high or low, as worthy or unworthy, which prevails in Mexico and the United States, is altogether wanting in Switzerland. If there exist class distinctions, they are such as may arise in a homogeneous society under the conditions of modern civilization, or they are a survival from the feudal age. They are not such as proceed from the co-existence in the population of members of different races regarded as inferior and superior. The illiteracy and general ignorance, moreover, which characterize a considerable part of the population both in Mexico and the United States, are also wanting in Switzerland; in fact, in no country of the world are the affairs of education administered more zealously or with greater efficiency. The problem of republican government is, therefore, simpler in Switzerland than in America, in spite of the proximity of the Swiss to the monarchial rule of European states.

CHAPTER II.

ANTECEDENTS OF SWISS FEDERALISM.

AMONG the many small republics of Europe which came into existence in the popular revolt from feudalism, those of Switzerland are conspicuous for the thoroughness and persistence of their republicanism. The lands whose union was the beginning of the Swiss Confederation held, before their alliance, a position in relation to the empire not greatly unlike that which the British colonies in America sustained towards the government of England. They acknowledged the supremacy of the empire, and it was no part of their early purpose to renounce this allegiance. The British colonies, also, in their first movement towards union, did not propose to sever their connection with the supreme government; they sought to control those affairs which, from their point of view, appeared to concern merely themselves. The conflicts which arose in the two cases had certain features in common. In each case it was a struggle between the spirit of feudal domination on the one side, and the spirit of democracy on the other. The primitive cantons directed their opposition, not against the supreme authority, but against the feudal lords who had acquired immediate suzerainty over them. So the British colonists, while they stoutly maintained their loyalty to the king and the English constitution, prepared with great determination to resist the governors who were sent among them. In the resistance offered by the people to the governors we observe the beginnings of a democratic war on feudalism. " The governors came over with high ideas of their own importance, and with not a little of the feudal spirit, which regarded the possessors of power as the holders of so much personal property that they might turn to their own private uses; while the assemblies were imbued with the spirit of the great idea that government is an agency or trust, which was to be exercised for the common good." [1] In spite of the professed loyalty of the cantons and the colonies, and their original determination to form unions without changing their relations with the supreme governments, they nevertheless, in both cases, assumed positions and established institu-

[1] Frothingham, " The Rise of the Republic of the United States," 127.

tions which were absolutely irreconcilable with the lingering feudalism that still found exponents in the emperor and the king.[1]

But the general circumstances under which liberty was developed in the two republics were different. In Switzerland it grew up in a population which, on the same soil, had been subjected to feudal rule. Among the British colonists of America, it grew on a new soil, in a field free from the embarrassing traditions of earlier social forms; in a field, moreover, whose population was in large part composed of those, or the descendants of those, who had fled from the disagreeable religious and political restraints of an older society. In the one case, liberty was developed in the immediate presence of rejected authority; in the other case, its growth was encouraged by the leveling influences of frontier life, and by a wide separation from the seat of the supreme power. The two subsequent phases of development in both cases were the same. Having obtained independence, a loose confederation was formed in each case, with a single assembly as the sole organ of confederate authority; and, as a third phase of political growth, the confederate congress was supplanted by a federal organization. In the United States, the transition was made in 1788; in Switzerland, in 1848.

[1] Frothingham, 161.

The first important event in the history of the Swiss republics was the union of Uri, Schwyz, and Unterwalden, in 1291. The movement by which this union was effected was not an isolated undertaking, but was in some sense characteristic of the age to which it belongs. Other phases of it are seen in the organization of city republics, and their attempts to acquire a recognition of their liberties; and in the formation of leagues of cities, like the Hanseatic League, or the League of the Rhine. At the time of their union, the lands which became the three primitive cantons of Switzerland had released themselves from all obligations to feudal superiors, and attained a position with respect to the empire essentially like that of the free cities of Central Europe. Uri acquired this position in the early part of the thirteenth century; Schwyz and Unterwalden, a little later; and since 1240, the practical independence of all three has rested on an unimpeachable legal foundation. Though practically independent, they remained directly subordinated to the empire, and neither their individual striving nor their united action aimed to libertate them from this position of subordination. The union was formed rather to maintain this relation and to check the encroachments of the House of Hapsburg.

After the death of Frederick II., in 1250, the

imperial power rapidly declined, and the dependent princes and estates of the empire sought on all sides to extend their dominion. When Rudolf of Hapsburg, whose hereditary lands embraced a part of the present territory of Switzerland, was made emperor in 1273, it was his weakness that chiefly recommended him to the electors. It was hoped that he would not be able to check the tendency to particularism that had been gaining strength during the previous quarter of a century. Rudolf occupied the throne for eighteen years, and died on the 15th of August, 1291. A few months before his death he purchased for his son, Duke Albrecht, certain rights of feudal jurisdiction over the city of Luzern and its outlying lands. The knowledge of Albrecht's zeal in enlarging the Hapsburg dominions made the free cities and cantons solicitous for the preservation of their liberties. Shortly after Rudolf's death, therefore, the citizens of Zurich, then a free city, resolved that the town "should not fall to any lord, except with the common consent of the community." A week later, on the 1st of August, Uri, Schwyz, and Unterwalden joined in a perpetual union, and adopted articles of confederation.[1]

[1] Bluntschli "Geschichte des schweizerischen Bundesrechtes," I, 59, 60; II, 1.

The parties to this alliance sought by means of it to be "better able to defend themselves and their property, and more readily to preserve them in their proper condition;" and to the attainment of this end they promised to coöperate with all their means and ability. To oppose all encroachments of enemies, they promised, moreover, to render aid, at their own expense, to any member of the Confederation according to its needs. Their oath involved a refusal to accept a judge who had purchased his office, or who did not belong to and reside in the canton. In case of strife arising within the Confederation, the more prudent men should step forward to allay the discord in such a manner as might seem to them most expedient; and if one party would not accept this mediation, the others acting together should enforce submission; and it should be the duty of all to uphold those charged with the enforcement of obedience. If a person should take the life of another, he should be executed, "if not able to show his innocence of the crime,"[1] and if perchance he had fled, he should never return. It was further provided that anyone who might succor and defend such a criminal should be banished from the lands of the Confederation until

[1] "Nisi suam de dicto maleficio valeat ostendere innocenciam." Art. 6.

he should be "deliberately recalled by the parties to this compact." The incendiary should be deprived of his civil and political rights, and the property of anyone who might succor or defend him should be confiscated for the satisfaction of the injured party. If anyone should deprive another of the allies of his property, or injure him in any way whatsoever, the property of the criminal should be confiscated and kept for the satisfaction of the person injured, in accordance with justice.

The formation of this union was the first step in the political development of Switzerland, and the articles of union became the historical basis of the republic. By it primitive political groups were permanently united, illustrating the first phase in the growth of a nation. By establishing certain relations between the united cantons and external powers, and by determining conditions of internal administration, it indicated the double field of sovereign activity which the republic was later to enter.

The second step was the enlargement of the union through the addition of five other confederates, joined to the original cantons by special treaties. In November, 1332, Luzern became the fourth member of the Confederation. This city was then under the suzerainty of Austria. It recognized its subordination, yet at the same time, in forming an alliance with the cantons, it acted in opposition to its legitimate superior. The alliance was the first step towards the rejection of Austrian supremacy. In May, 1351, Zurich united in a perpetual union with Luzern and the three cantons. Its wealth and important position as a free imperial city gave it great influence among the allies, yet it held no legal superiority. The next year Glarus and Zug were added, and in March, 1353, by the alliance of Bern, the union reached a point of its growth in numbers at which it remained for one hundred and twenty-eight years, till 1481. The period which ended here was the heroic age of Switzerland. At Morgarten (1315), Sempach (1386), and Näfles (1387), the Swiss people gave unmistakable evidence of a determination in favor of liberty.

The third step was marked by the addition of five other members. Bern had retained in the Confederation her own policy; and her efforts to range the other cities, Zurich and Luzern, on her side, were so far successful that there appeared a city party and a country party. This divergence of policy was, however, in a measure the outgrowth of different social and political conditions. In the one case the people lived in isolated dwellings, scattered along the valleys and over the sides of mountains; in the other case they were confined to the narrow limits of crowded cities. The constitutions of the rural cantons were strongly democratic; those of the cities were aristocratic. The most important feature of the government in one case was an assembly of all the freemen; in the other case, a council of distinguished citizens. When Freiburg and Solothurn sought admission, the two parties found opportunity to express their antagonistic views. The cities favored the application, while the rural cantons opposed it. It was clearly seen that the proposed enlargement of the Confederation involved a still more complete transfer of the balance of power to the cities; and this fact, which was for the rural cantons a ground of opposition, was for the cities the basis of their advocacy. In 1477 the three cities formed a perpetual alliance with Freiburg and Solothurn, and this act only added intensity to the jealousy and indignation of the rural cantons. A breach between the parties appeared imminent, but was averted by the agreement effected at Stantz, in December, 1481. By this agreement the members of the Confederation engaged to use no violence towards one another, nor to allow violence to be used by their dependents, but to aid one another in bringing their refractory subjects to obedience. At this meeting also party strife was allayed, and Friburg and Stolohurn were admitted to membership in the Confederation. Twenty years later, in 1501, the cities of Basel and Schaffhausen were added, and in 1513 the canton of Appenzell. After the admission of Appenzell, no further increase in the membership of the Confederacy was made for nearly three hundred years, till 1798.

In these early steps towards the formation of a national government, the Confederation had to determine two points: (1) Its ability to preserve its independence against encroachments from without; (2) its ability to maintain a lasting union of its several parts. The first point was practically determined by "the eight old cantons." When, however, the number of confederates had been increased to thirteen, and the danger of being overwhelmed by hostile neighbors had been set aside, the forces of internal discord became manifest. To the social and political differences which appeared in the contrast between the city and rural cantons, there were added, as a consequence of the Reformation, the antagonisms of different religious creeds, subjecting the Confederation to a strain that threatened to destroy it. This was the critical period in the development of the Swiss Republic; for the preservation of liberty was dependent on the preservation of union.

Between the admission of Appenzell, in 1513, and the establishment of the Helvetic Republic, in 1798, the number of members in the Confederation remained unchanged. It does not follow from this fact, however, that the amount of territory under Swiss dominion remained unchanged. On the contrary, it was considerably enlarged, and that chiefly in two ways: (1) Through acquisitions by individual cantons; (2) through alliances, in which the Confederation, or a canton, or several cantons together, retained a superior position, while the other parties to the compact held subordinate positions. Before the end of the sixteenth century, a number of cities, rural communes, and small principalities had fallen into this list.

These subordinate allies were not actual members of the Confederation, but through their connections with some or all of the cantons, they participated in the fate of the whole. Although the early alliances out of which the completed Confederation grew were formed with no design of opposing the authority of the empire, yet long before the independence of the Confederation was formally acknowledged by the European nations, through the Treaty of Westphalia, it had attained to practical independence, and to the exercise of the powers of a sovereign state. As an independent state, Switzerland has held two positions with respect to the international politics of Europe : that of an ally, and that of a neutral. As an ally, the Swiss achieved more military glory than political advantage. " The first time they interfered on a large scale in foreign affairs, they were disgracefully misused, and inflicted upon themselves the greatest injuries. Their military victories were at the same time political defeats. Without any grievance of their own, led away entirely by foreign suggestion and foreign money, they undertook the war against Charles the Bold. And while they broke the power of the Burgundian duke without appreciating how completely they were acting in the interest of the French king, they destroyed an important middle power not only between France and Switzerland, but also between France and Austria. Had the Duke of Burgundy retained essentially his position, Switzerland as a consequence would have won in him a natural ally in opposition to the great powers of France and Austria, and much friction between these two powers would have been prevented. But for the sake of temporary advantages, the Swiss overlooked the lasting interests of their independence and peace. After this they fell more and more under the influence of the French policy, and were more completely subjected than before to the fluctuations produced by the nearness of France to Austria."[1]

The rôle which they played in the Italian wars was scarcely more to their credit or advantage, although at one time the fate of the duchy of Milan was practically in their hands, and they were momentarily moved by the ambition to win for themselves a place among the great powers of Europe. They were, however, not organized for conquest, nor were they the chief representatives of any one of the great peoples of the Continent. They became conscious of these facts, and recognized that their military renown had been gained chiefly in struggles for their liberty and independence, and that it was the maintenance of these which constituted the proper end of their military activity.

As long as the Confederation was surrounded by unfriendly neighbors, its unity was secured by the force of external pressure. The first serious danger of dissolution overtook it when it had made peace with all the world, and found opportunity to develop internal antagonisms. The early contrasts presented by town and country aroused for a time the spirit of disunion, but the attitude of neighboring powers furnished a superior reason for united action. Yet when

[1] Bluntschli, I, 265.

ANTECEDENTS OF SWISS FEDERALISM. 23

the Reformation had thrown among the people the fire-brand of ecclesiastical controversy, an explosion appeared imminent. Under the influence of an antagonism of creeds, the old order of things was so far broken up that there appeared one diet for the Catholic cantons and another for the Prostestant cantons. Gradually, however, the breach was healed, and a single body continued to act for the whole Confederation.

The Diet of the thirteen cantons was the sole organ of the Confederation. In the earlier times it had no definitely fixed form nor fixed times and place of meeting. Besides the assembly of delegates from all the cantons, there were assemblies of delegates from only such cantons as were concerned in the business to be brought forward, and after the Reformation, meetings of the Catholic and Protestant cantons separately. The meetings of the Diet were held "at the most diverse times of the year, as the business to be transacted demanded, and lasted usually only one or a few days, but were easily and often repeated, so that in a single year there often occurred a whole series of different sessions."[1] Later, the place and time of meeting were both prescribed, and at a single session the business of the whole year was

[1] Bluntschli, I, 392.

considered. At first, any canton might summon the Diet, but later it was provided that the regular call for a meeting should be made through the *Vorort*, Zurich. Each canton, still, in the sixteenth century, often sent only one delegate; after this, however, it became customary to send two, yet there was no legal determination of the number it might send. It was, in fact, a matter of slight importance, inasmuch as the voting was not by persons but by cantons, each canton having one vote, without regard to the extent of its territory or the amount of its population. The subordinate estates, however, that were represented in the Diet, the abbot of St. Gallen, the city of St. Gallen, and the city of Bienne, were not permitted to send more than one delegate. The powers of the Diet were not those of a representative body, but rather those of an assembly of ambassadors, in which each member acted according to instructions given by his superior. But the assembly was not limited to a prescribed circle of activity; it was competent to discuss all matters of interest to the Confederation. It was the medium through which all negotiations between the Confederation and other states were carried on. "It received the ambassadors of foreign powers, listened to their addresses, and made reply; it also sent ambassadors now and then to foreign countries. It made war and peace in the name of the Confederation; and in the case of war between neighboring powers, it made the necessary provisions for defending its territory and neutrality. It negotiated alliances with foreign states, which each canton, however, remained at liberty to accept or reject."[1] Yet no canton was at liberty to conclude alliances with foreign states without the consent of the Diet. But the fact that ambassadors were received by the Diet did not prevent them from being accredited to, and received by, the individual cantons. The Confederation had no resident ministers at foreign courts, but sent ambassadors as the occasion seemed to demand. This power was also exercised by the several cantons, and it sometimes happened that a number of cantons had ambassadors near the same court at the same time; and in the case of the renewal of the alliance with France, each of the cantons had its representative near the French court.

In order that the Confederation might be in a position to exert upon its neighbors either a moral or a physical influence, it was necessary that internal harmony should prevail; and the task of securing this state of things fell upon the

[1] Blumer, "Handbuch des schweizerischen Bundesstaatsrechtes," I, 14.

Diet as the only organ of the united cantons. Not having the powers of a sovereign over subordinate societies, the Diet was obliged to rely chiefly on mediation; and it regarded interference by this means a duty, even when not appealed to by the parties in conflict. The chief weakness of the Confederation with respect to internal affairs lay in the fact that the principle of majority rule was adopted only to a very limited extent. Each canton voted with perfect freedom, and was not obliged usually to follow the decision of the others. In the course of time it came to be accepted that the minority should accede to the will of the majority, in cases where the articles of union or special agreements of all concerned gave the majority the right to form conclusions. The acceptance of this principle was a consequence of a growing sense of common interests and a common destiny, coupled with the conviction that no one canton should be allowed, through its stubbornness, to jeopardize the well-being of the whole.

The early history of Switzerland shows no more unity in military than in civil affairs. "Each individual canton had a military organization of its own. And when a common war was undertaken by the Confederation, each canton sent its troops under its own standard and under officers appointed by itself."[1] The army

[1] Bluntschli, I, 409.

thus constituted had no single officer in supreme command. The plans of campaigns and of battles were evolved and adopted by the chief officers in council. Sometimes the soldiers of the cantons were attended in the field by several members of the cantonal councils, who participated in the discussion of affairs, and formed, as it were, a diet in the field. Sometimes, also, the members of the councils, the officers, and the whole army, met for deliberation in a great confederate assembly. These provisions for the control of the army were necessarily found inefficient. The exigencies of war demanded a centralization of authority, and for great emergencies and for the overcoming of peculiar difficulties, a single officer was given the supreme command, either by the direct action of the Diet, or by the action of the chief cantonal officers, or by the action of a single canton authorized by the Diet. In such cases the military leadership was likely to fall to the canton that enjoyed political preeminence.

The sixteenth century, with its ecclesiastical antagonisms, threatened the Confederation with dissolution; but during the next century a strong reactionary tendency was manifest, and European states sought to realize the principles of absolutism in their organizations. In so far as this movement affected Switzerland, it emphasized the need of centralization. Its effect in Germany was to make the States of the empire imitate the absolutism of France. It thus weakened their support of the central power. The Thirty Years' War and the encroachments of France on her neighbors made the Swiss feel more than ever the need of a common agent of defense. An important step towards the creation of such an agent was the establishment of the Defensional, first brought forward in 1629, but not fully carried out till during the wars of Louis XIV., in 1668. Under the provisions of this agreement, adopted unanimously by the Diet, each canton was required to hold itself in readiness to furnish, whenever they should be called for, a certain number of men and a certain amount of munitions. The total number of men provided for was forty thousand and two hundred, in three divisions of thirteen thousand four hundred each. Of each of the three divisions Zurich was to provide fourteen hundred men, Bern two thousand, Luzern twelve hundred, the Abbot of St. Gallen one thousand, and the other cantons different numbers, ranging from one hundred to eight hundred. The second and third divisions were of the same size, and to be furnished in the same way.

In spite of this attempt to form an effective union for defense, the indifference and mutual jealousy of the several cantons rendered the Confederation practically defenseless and made its disruption by a foreign power an easy task. Throughout the seventeenth and eighteenth centuries, the aristocratic elements had increased at the expense of the democratic, and against this dominant aristocracy the French democracy directed its propagandism. It prevailed here, backed by the French army, as it had prevailed in Holland and Italy. Overwhelmed by the French forces, there was no alternative for the cantons but to submit to the dictation of their conquerors; and thus, in violation of their history and traditions, there was established the Helvetic Republic, a centralized state modeled after the republican government then existing in France.

This was the fourth step towards the formation of a national administration for Switzerland. It was a complete revolution in both the form and the theory of the government. Whatever had existed hitherto was the product of a growth along historical lines, in which ancient traditional rights had been preserved, and the sovereignty of the several cantons had remained inviolate. Under the constitution of 1798, established through the interference of France, the historical ground was abandoned, and a basis was sought in the doctrine of natural right. The cantons were deprived of their independence, and there was set up a "representative democracy resting on the abstract ideas of liberty, equality, and popular sovereignty."[1]

The characteristic features of the new constitution were the following: "The sovereignty resided simply and solely in the totality of the citizens of the Helvetic Republic as an indissoluble state, in which the cantons formed merely administrative districts. The people exercised its sovereignty, however, only in adopting the constitution and in appointing electors, in the primary assemblies, one for each one hundred active citizens. The electors of each canton assembled for the election of the deputies of the two Houses of the Legislature, the members of the cantonal courts, and of the bureaux of administration. The legislative power of the republic was exercised by the Great Council, which at first consisted of eight deputies from each canton, but afterwards was to be constituted with reference to the population, and by the Senate, composed of those who had held the office of director, and of four deputies from each canton, who were required to be thirty years old, to be married or widowers, and to have already held some one or more of the higher offices. The

[1] Blumer, I, 19; Bluntschli, II, 305–322, for the constitution of 1798.

Senate was empowered to accept or reject bills passed by the Great Council. The two councils elected the executive Directory of five members, the manner of election being, that for each place to be filled one of the councils, determined by lot, formed a list of five candidates, from which the other council named the Director. The Directory, supported by four ministers designated by itself for the different departments of the administration, was the proper 'government' of Switzerland. Its organs were the stadtholders in the cantons, the under-stadtholders in the districts, and the agents in the communes. The affairs peculiar to the cantons found certain, although inadequate, consideration in the bureaux of administration, which were charged with the immediate execution of the laws relating to finance and trade, art, labor, agriculture, food, the maintenance of the cities, and country roads. The administration of justice was carried on through district and cantonal courts and one supreme court. The last, consisting of one member from each canton, tried cases involving charges against the members of the legislature and the executive, decided in the second instance important criminal cases, and was empowered to set aside the decisions of the lower courts in civil cases on account of technical informalities, want of competence, or violation of the constitution. The division into cantons maintained for the most part the boundaries of the former confederated cantons and the subordinate lands; yet the extensive territory of the republic of Bern was divided into four new cantons: Bern, Oberland, Aargau, and Leman; while on the other hand the three original cantons were united with Zug, forming the new canton of Waldstätten. Glarus, Gaster, Uznach, Rapperschwyl, Upper Toggenberg, Sax, Gams, Werdenberg, and Sorgans were united in the new canton of Linth; and Appenzell, the city and land of St. Gallen, the Rheinthal, and Lower Toggenberg formed the new canton of Säntis. The avowed purpose of this transformation in interior and eastern Switzerland was to weaken the old democracies, which appeared as the seat of the opposition to the new order of things."[1]

The adoption of this constitution was a long step away from the previously existing loose confederation, towards a centralized state. It was a longer step than the Swiss were prepared to take alone. The form of government imposed upon them was in no sense an expression of the degree of political progress which they had made. The Helvetic Directory acted under instructions from Paris, and its pretensions to independence were a hollow sham. Switzer-

---

[1] Bumerl I, 19, 20.

land was forced into an alliance with the French Republic, and was obliged to see her lands overrun and her treasure carried off by the troops of her ally. The constitution of 1798 was created by the Directory of France, and had to be upheld by its creator. Its existence was, therefore, terminated by the fall of the Directory. It lasted long enough, however, to make on the minds of a considerable part of the population an impression favorable to a more centralized government than had hitherto existed; and when it ceased to be in force, in the beginning of 1800, it left the Swiss divided into two parties, the Centralists and the Federalists. The Federalists adhered to ancient traditions and sought to revive the old Confederation. The Centralists, on the other hand, had come into existence under the Helvetic Republic, and were the advocates of centralization. The political events of Switzerland during the following three years were strongly colored by the contentions of these two parties.

The crisis in France, through which the Directory was supplanted by the Consulate, showed a drift of power towards a single point in the organism. But the strength of the Federalist party made it impossible for Switzerland, of her own will, to follow the lead of France in this direction; and the First Consul, however arbitrary his dealings with the Swiss, manifested no desire to divert them from the course of development marked out by their historical traditions. On the contrary, he pointed out the fact that what they needed was a federal constitution, "equality of rights between the cantons, a renunciation of all family privileges, and the independent organization of each canton." To frame for themselves a constitution was then the task immediately at hand; and in the meantime, while the task remained unfinished, the powers of the state rested in a provisional government, consisting of a legislative council of fifty members and an executive council of seven members. During this period of transition several constitutions were formed, but inasmuch as they were formed under the dominance of those influences which had determined the character of the constitution of 1798, they for the most part emphasized the scheme of centralization embodied in that instrument. They were all, however, either still-born or had only a brief and hopeless existence. But these unsuccessful attempts indicate that, during the years of agitation and confusion produced by foreign interference, the national idea had gained in strength and clearness. It was no longer possible to go back to the old organization. Even the Federalists, who insisted on organizing the state as a Union of more or less independent cantons, saw clearly the need of greater centralization than had existed under the old Confederation.

As long as French troops occupied the country, the Centralists kept the upper hand. But in 1802, after the treaty of Amiens, these troops were withdrawn. This left both parties without foreign support, and also without foreign restraint. Although the Swiss had had democratic institutions for some centuries, yet, in reference to questions of general concern, the minority had not learned to submit peaceably to the majority. Party conflicts over these matters, therefore, meant civil war. Through foreign intervention, the Swiss had been placed in a position from which they seemed to be unable to extricate themselves, and it is not to be supposed that in withdrawing his army Napoleon intended to leave them to work out their own salvation alone. He had become indispensable to them, and he wished the fact to be recognized. The uproar and confusion produced by the contending parties after his withdrawal, gave him the desired opportunity to appear as a mediator. He again sent an army into Switzerland, commanded a cessation of hostilities, and called delegates of both parties to meet him in Paris, for the purpose of discussing the fundamental principles of a new constitution. In the conference which followed he showed a remarkably clear and just comprehension of the real needs of the people for whom he proposed to legislate. In spite of his identification with the movement towards unity in France, he decided with great definiteness of opinion in favor of federation for Switzerland; and it must be set down as evidence of his political insight that he indicated, as desirable for the Swiss, a position among the nations essentially the same as that which they hold at the present time.

The result of this conference was the Act of Mediation, a fundamental law which marks the fifth phase of the governmental history of Switzerland. Its promulgation put an end to the hopeless attempt to transform the loose alliance into a centralized state, and established federalism as the principle of subsequent political growth. The number of cantons was increased from thirteen to nineteen. Those previously existing retained their ancient limits, except that Aargau and Vaud were composed in part of territory taken from Bern. The constitutions of the democratic cantons were restored, modified only with respect to the age required by voters, and with respect to the initiative in legislation. The six new cantons were: (1) St. Gallen, consisting of the city of St. Gallen, the territory of the former abbey of St.

ANTECEDENTS OF SWISS FEDERALISM. 37

Gallen, and the districts of Rheinthal, Sax, Gams, Werdenberg, Sargans, Gaster, Uznach, and Rapperschwyl; (2) Granbünden, comprising most of the territory of the three Rhæitan unions; (3) Aargau, made up in part of territory which formerly belonged to Bern, and in part of territory acquired from Austria ; (4) Thurgau; (5) Ticino, embracing the Italian possessions; (6) Vaud, comprising lands formerly belonging to Bern and Freiburg. Of these Granbünden retained its ancient constitution, modified only in certain particulars to adapt it to its new circumstances. The other new cantons, Aargau, St. Gallen, Ticino, Thurgau, and Vaud, received constitutions providing for a system of representation, but a system in which the method of election was even more complicated than in the city cantons. As to the manner of election, the members of the great council were divided into three classes. The members of the first third were elected by a direct election from certain districts, the only qualification being that the candidates should be thirty years of age. "For the other two-thirds, lists of the candidates were formed from other districts, and, indeed, according to two different principles, that of wealth and that of age. For the second third a considerably higher property qualification was demanded than in the other cantons; on the other hand, for this class the age of twenty-five was adequate. The members of the last third were required to be at least fifty years of age, and at the same time to possess a certain amount of property. From the list of candidates thus formed from rich and old men, the actual members of the great council were drawn by lot."[1] Inasmuch as these cantons had not hitherto enjoyed equal rights of membership in the Confederation with those that had been admitted before the Revolution, Napoleon was able to deal with them freely without interfering with any rights that had been sanctioned by time.

The period of centralization under the constitution of 1798, however brief and stormy, undoubtedly removed to a certain extent the ancient jealousy of the cantons of one another, and made them less reluctant than formerly to accord to a central power the control of common affairs. The interference of Napoleon thus initiated on the part of the cantons the habit of looking to a superior to whom they all held a common relation; and in so far as this had any bearing on their political development, it brought them into a more favorable position for accepting the plan of a federal organization. The cantons " mutually guaranteed to one another their

[1] Bluntschli, I, 469; Blumer, I, 36.

constitutions, their territories, and their freedom and independence, not only against foreign powers but also against the encroachments of other cantons and individual factions." Under the Act of Mediation, moreover, there were established certain fundamental provisions : (1) There should be no more lands subordinated to the cantons, those previously existing having been made cantons in the Confederation; (2) all privileges of place or of birth, whether of single persons or of families, should be set aside; (3) any Swiss should be allowed to settle freely in any canton; (4) no internal duties should be collected and no impediment should be put in the way of the free circulation of food, live stock, and merchandise; (5) the Diet should establish a proper standard of coinage ; (6) no canton should afford refuge and protection to criminals fleeing from other cantons, and no exception under this provision should be made in favor of political offenders ; (7) cantons should not form alliances among themselves nor with foreign powers ; (8) cantonal authorities should be held responsible for their violations of laws established by the Confederation, and the complaints in such cases should be brought before a tribunal composed of the presidents of the criminal courts of the cantons not under accusation.

These specifications indicate that the cantons

had lost somewhat of that complete independence which they had enjoyed before the Revolution; and this loss by the parts implied a gain by some organ or agent of the whole. The central organization which came into existence through this revolution still bore marks of cantonal jealousy, as seen in the fact that the seat of the central authority was changed from year to year, being temporarily established in succession at Freiburg, Bern, Solothurn, Basel, Zurich, and Luzern, each of the cantons here named taking in turn the position of Directorial Canton. The chief magistrate of the Directorial Canton became, for the time being, the head of the Confederation, with the title of Landamman of Switzerland. He retained his position in the canton, however, and at the same time stood as the representative of the national organization. He kept the seal of the republic, received foreign ambassadors, conducted diplomatic negotiations, laid before the Diet the necessary communications on the affairs of the Union, and with the consent of the government of the Directorial Canton disposed the troops in the interests of internal order. Without his consent no canton could raise more than five hundred soldiers. In case of conflict between cantons, he could provide for a settlement of the matter by appointing an arbiter, or by referring it to the next session of the Diet. He warned the cantons of threatening danger. He supervised certain departments of public works, as streets, roads, and improvement of river beds. As the head of a state which still had many of the features of a loose confederacy, many of the functions of the Landamman were those of a mediator.

In spite of the loss of certain functions, the Diet under the Act of Mediation retained many of the characteristic features of the Diet of the thirteen cantons. Like that body, it was an assembly of ambassadors, not of representatives. As in that body, moreover, the members of this acted on instructions from the cantons which had sent them. Instead of each canton having one vote, however, as formerly, those of over one hundred thousand inhabitants, as Bern, Zurich, Vaud, St. Gallen, Aargau, and Graubünden, now had two. Yet in spite of this provision, Bluntschli says that "external equality of all the cantons remained the fundamental principle." The Diet was empowered to declare war, make peace, and conclude alliances, but decisions in these matters to be valid required the assent of three-fourths of the members. The Diet had, moreover, the authority to make commercial treaties, and military capitulations. It exercised control over the cantonal contingents of the troops, appointed the general of the army, and took such measures as were necessary to the security and peace of the country. It decided in cases of conflict between cantons, when the mediator could not solve the difficulty, but in these cases the members pronounced judgment freely without instructions.

There were also involved in the central government a chancellor and a secretary, elected by the Diet for a period of two years; but inasmuch as they were eligible for re-election, they were usually continued in office for a number of successive terms. They were paid by the Directorial Canton, as was also the Landamman of Switzerland.

During the period in which this constitution continued in force, Switzerland enjoyed unusual peace and prosperity. It entered into a close alliance with France, through which certain commercial and military advantages were to accrue to the two nations. By a later military capitulation, France was permitted to enroll sixteen thousand Swiss in her army, but by a treaty formed in 1812 the number was limited to twelve thousand. Although Napoleon acknowledged the complete independence of Switzerland, yet France under him exercised over it the powers of a protectorate. Herein lay an unfortunate circumstance for the republic. The new constitution satisfied fairly well the political wants of the Swiss people, but it had come to be regarded not as an expression of an independent European power, but as a contrivance of the First Consul imposed upon the nation. In the public mind of Europe it became identified with the interests of the French Government, and by this means it became exposed to the suspicion and hatred of the Allies to such an extent that the fall of Napoleon necessarily carried with it the overthrow of this piece of his handiwork.

Soon after the defeat of Napoleon at Leipsic, in 1813, the Allies invaded the territory of Switzerland, and in December the Swiss Diet met at Zurich and formally set aside the Act of Mediation. At the same time it declared in favor of retaining the new cantons in the Confederation; in favor of providing a constitution which should embrace all the cantons in a common union; and in opposition to holding any cities or lands in a subject relation. The reactionary party rejected these propositions, and under the leadership of Bern sought a revival of pre-revolutionary conditions, and demanded that a diet of the thirteen cantons should be convoked as the only legitimate power in the 'Confederation. Zurich and her followers held to the Confederation in its largest and latest extent, while the reactionary party withdrew and called a diet of the "eight old cantons." "This outward separation was, however, soon abolished by the pointed declaration of the foreign ambassadors, that the Allies had determined irrevocably to preserve the integrity and independence of all the nineteen cantons, and would recognize no other diet than that assembled at Zurich."[1] On the 6th of April, 1814, the Diet at Zurich embraced delegates from all of the nineteen cantons. The actual antagonisms, however, were not allayed, yet the opposing parties were placed in such relations to one another that it was possible for them to work towards union. The questions at issue had reference chiefly to the position that should be accorded to the new cantons, and to the amount of power that should be given to the central organization. The democratic cantons wished as complete local sovereignty as possible, and their opposition made it necessary to relinquish much that had been won for centralization since 1798.

The disappearance of Napoleon from the political field left Switzerland in somewhat intimate relations with the victorious Allies. They were disposed, however, to leave the Confederation free to work out the details of its internal organization, only requiring certain general conditions to be fulfilled. In the first treaty of Paris, in 1814, it was stated that "Switzerland as an in-

[1] Blumer, I, 46.

ANTECEDENTS OF SWISS FEDERALISM. 45

dependent state will continue to govern itself." In order to remove the conflicts between the cantons regarding their territorial limits, the Congress of Vienna invited the Swiss to send ambassadors to Vienna, to treat with the representatives of the allied powers there assembled. The Congress then laid before the Swiss ambassadors certain propositions, on the acceptance of which the Allies promised to extend to Switzerland a formal and legal recognition of her perpetual neutrality. These propositions were: (1) That the nineteen cantons, as they stood on the 13th of December, 1813, should continue as the basis of the Confederation; (2) that Wallis, the territory of Geneva, and the principality of Neufchâtel, should be embodied in Switzerland as three new cantons; (3) that the bishopric of Basel should be added to the cantons of Bern and Basel, and the city of Bienne to the canton of Bern; (4) that the territorial claims of Schwyz, Unterwalden, Uri, Glarus, Zug, and Appenzell against Aargau, Vaud, Ticino, and St. Gallen should be met by the payment by the latter cantons of five hundred thousand francs; (5) that a yearly stipend should be fixed for the Abbot of St. Gallen. These propositions were accepted, and Switzerland received from Austria, Spain, France, Great Britain, Portugal, Prussia, Russia, and Sweden the desired documentary guarantee of her perpetual neutrality. As in the Treaty of Westphalia, after the Thirty Years' War, the powers of Europe recognized Switzerland's independence of the empire long after it had been established as a fact, so here at the close of the Napoleonic wars the powers represented in the Congress of Vienna acknowledged the neutrality of Switzerland, which, according to the Swiss view, was a recognition of what had long existed in fact, and of a principle that had long been fundamental in Swiss politics.

After much wrangling and hesitating, a new constitution for the Confederation was completed, and finally accepted by the twenty-two cantons, August 7, 1815. As compared with the Act of Mediation, it laid little stress on the central authority. Under the preceding organization the individual cantons recognized their obligations to conform themselves to the principles of the federal law, and it was definitely stated in the Act of Mediation that the cantons should exercise all those powers which had not been expressly delegated to the federal authority. But in the constitution of 1815, limitations on cantonal sovereignty were made less conspicuous. The cantons are described as united for the "maintenance of their liberty, independence, and security against the attacks of foreign powers and the preservation of internal peace and order." They mutually guaranteed their constitutions and their territories. They provided for a common military force of two men from each one hundred of the population. They established the principle of arbitration for settling intercantonal disputes, prohibited the existence of subject lands as they had previously existed, and determined that the several cantons should form no alliances detrimental to the Union or to any canton. But alliances between cantons were not definitely prohibited, as they had been by the Act of Mediation, nor were the several cantons prohibited from making certain military capitulations and treaties on commercial affairs and on police affairs with foreign powers, but it was required that such treaties having been made they should be reported to the Diet. " The Act of Mediation did not by any means organize Switzerland as a *Bundesstaat*, but there was in the Landamman a standing central organ through which a series of measures for the protection of the common interests could be carried out. The essential character of the new articles of union lay in this, that they made the Confederation once more purely a *Staatenbund*, placed the sovereignty in the cantons, and made no mention whatever of the central power, or at least crowded it into the background." [1]

[1] Von Orelli, "Das Staatsrecht der schweizerischen Eidgenossenschaft," 19.

Under this constitution, " the enjoyment of political rights was never to become the exclusive privilege of a class of the citizens of a canton." Moreover, the inequality of cantonal representation in the Diet, which had existed under the Act of Mediation, was set aside, and the ancient equality restored, in spite of the vigorous opposition of the larger cantons. Each canton had one vote; still, the superior moral weight of the larger cantons made itself felt on the course of events. The ambassadors of the cantons in the Diet voted, as previously, according to instructions; but, in contrast with the previous condition of things, the principle of majority rule was gradually gaining acceptance. In certain cases, however, such as decisions relative to war and peace, and alliances with foreign states, the specified majority of three-fourths required under the Act of Mediation was here continued. The powers delegated to the Diet extended to the formation of commercial treaties with foreign states, the appointment of ambassadors, the determination of the organization of the troops, the control of the army, the appointment of the generals, the officers of the general staff, and the colonels of the confederate army, the supervision of the discipline and equipment of the troops, and to all measures for the external and internal security of the Confederation.

ANTECEDENTS OF SWISS FEDERALISM. 49

The office of Landamman of Switzerland fell with the Act of Mediation. It became necessary, therefore, to provide an organ for the administration of general affairs between the sessions of the Diet. It was proposed to make Zurich the sole *Vorort*, and her burgermeister the president of the Diet and of the Confederation; and to intrust him with the daily correspondence and the current business of the general administration. This proposition, however, together with all the provisions of detail depending upon it, failed of acceptance. Bern opposed with special vigor the plan to make Zurich the sole *Vorort*. It was finally determined to make three cities, Zurich, Bern, and Luzern, in turn the seat of the general government, each exercising for a period of two years the powers of the *Vorort* before 1798. The burgermeister of the *Vorort* stood at the head of the confederate administration, but under certain circumstances the Diet might commission a body of six representatives, one from each of six groups of cantons, to take in charge the affairs of the Confederation. These representatives received instructions from the Diet, which determined the period of their activity. In any case their power ceased at the reassembling of the Diet. The agreement of two-thirds of the members was necessary to authoritative action.

They were paid from the treasury of the Confederation. Besides these arrangements for a central administration, it was also provided that the general secretaryship, as it had existed under the Act of Mediation, should be continued.

The constitution of 1815 was at best only a compromise between interests more or less antagonistic; and the fact that the Swiss people lived in peace and quiet under it for fifteen years is not necessarily to be taken as evidence of its adaptation to their political wants. The political peace following the Revolution was rather the result of a reaction from specially troubled times, under the revived force of cantonal traditions. During this period political activity was almost exclusively confined to the affairs of the cantons, in several of which new constitutions were framed and adopted. These new constitutions involved important fundamental principles. They recognized popular sovereignty, limiting its exercise to making elections and adopting or rejecting proposed amendments of the constitution. They transferred to the great council the power of making laws, of levying taxes, of instructing delegates to the Diet, and of supervising the general administration and the administration of justice. They removed the previously existing legal inequality between the cities and the rural districts, yet in some cases favored the capital towns with respect to representation. They established in most cases the direct popular election of members of the great council; provided for short terms of office; separated the judicial from the executive power, ordered freedom of the press and the right of petition; and in many of the cantons pledged the authorities to improve the public instruction.

Down to 1830, except during some portion of the Revolutionary period, the several cantons had been regarded as independent political societies. The articles of union were of their own creation, and became binding on any canton only by its voluntary action. The doctrine of State rights was accepted without question. On the 27th of December, 1830, the Diet declared "that every canton in the Confederation, by virtue of its sovereignty, was free to undertake such changes in the cantonal constitution as might appear to it desirable, in so far as these changes were not in opposition to the articles of union, and that the Diet would not interfere in any manner in such constitutional reforms as had already been made or even proposed." The adoption by the Diet of a policy of non-interference, left the cantons without any sufficient guarantee for their constitutions. The desire for such a guarantee, however, coupled with the inefficiency of the Diet, led to the establishment of new alliances for this purpose in different groups of cantons. In the spring of 1832, the seven cantons of Luzern, Zurich, Bern, Solothurn, St. Gallen, Aargau, and Thurgau, agreed mutually to guarantee their constitutions, and pledged themselves, in case strife should arise among them, to exercise the office of mediators and to secure to one another protection by force of arms. This was the first *Sonderbund* within the Confederation, and a prelude to the later unions and the so-called War of the Sonderbund. Besides aiming to furnish mutual security, it was also an attempt on the part of the then dominant radical-liberal party to form a more compact and effective organization in these cantons. This action of the seven liberal cantons was followed not long afterwards by the formation of the League of Sarnen, embracing Uri, Schwyz, Unterwalden, Wallis, and the city of Basel, in which the conservative party was dominant. The members of this union withdrew from the Diet, but the remaining cantons, acting through the existing general organization, raised an army of twenty thousand men, compelled them to dissolve their separate alliance, re-enter the Diet, and recognize the division of Basel into two half-cantons. The formation of these separate unions emphasized the existing party differences, and made apparent the need of a more efficient central authority.

The project to revise the articles of 1815 had already been several years under discussion, when the League of Sarnen was overthrown in 1833, and the results of these discussions showed a marked bias in favor of increasing the power of the central organization, and of establishing a genuine federal government. The draft of a federal constitution which was submitted to the popular vote in the summer of 1833 had been formed under the influence of the liberal party, and consequently met with an opposition from the side of the conservative or reactionary cantons, which made its adoption impossible. Later, party differences were increased by involving religious differences, and in 1846 the Confederation went asunder, the Catholic cantons becoming united in a separate union, which was virtually a revival of the League of Sarnen. An immediate object of this union was to defend the cause of the Jesuits, whom the Liberals wished expelled from the Confederation, as the cause of the recent internal troubles. Both parties soon went beyond the point where compromise was possible, and Switzerland became divided into two hostile camps. The Catholic cantons in the union, disregarding the articles of confederation of 1815, had "engaged to defend each other by an armed force, and appointed a council of war to concert all necessary measures for joint action." But their defeat was a foregone conclusion. Their army comprised about 50,000 men, while that of the Confederation was twice as large. The Confederation, moreover, had a superior moral support in that it represented the national idea. The triumph of the national-liberal party, which came speedily and without great effort, prepared the way for a new constitution.

The business of revising the constitution was taken up in earnest by a commission in February, 1848. This commission was composed of the first of each canton's ambassadors at the Diet, and all the cantons and half-cantons were represented, except Neufchâtel and Appenezll-Interior. In May the work of the commission was finished, and the draft of the constitution was brought before the Diet, where it was carefully discussed and amended, and finally submitted to the several cantons. Fifteen and a half cantons voted to accept it.[1] These affirmative

[1] These were: Zurich, Bern, Luzern, Glarus, Freiburg, Solothurn, Basel, Schaffhausen, Appenzell-Exterior, St. Gallen, Graubünden, Aargau, Thurgau, Vaud, Neufchâtel, and Geneva. The fourteen and a half cantons which voted for the amendments of 1874 were: Zurich, Bern, Glarus, Solothurn, Basel, Schaffhausen, Appenzell-Exterior, St. Gallen, Graubünden, Aargau, Thurgau, Ticino, Vaud, Neufchâtel, and Geneva.

votes embraced not only a majority of all the cantons, but also a large majority of the Swiss citizens. On the 12th of September, the Diet announced that the constitution had been adopted, and invited the several cantons to elect members of the two legislative assemblies. All of the cantons without exception acceded to the will of the majority, and acted in accordance with the invitation of the Diet. By these steps a federal government was put in the place of the previously existing unstable union of cantons; and the organization thus established has been maintained till the present time without fundamental modification. The changes of 1865 and 1874 were in the form of necessary extensions of the constitutional law. In the great reform of 1848, Switzerland was specially favored by the revolutionary movement of the time, which engaged the attention of her neighbors, and by the measurably successful example of a federal republic in America.

CHAPTER III.

THE DISTRIBUTION OF POWER.

LIKE the constitutions of the federal republics of Mexico, Venezuela, and Argentine, and unlike those of Colombia and the United States, the Swiss constitution begins by invoking the name of God. Then, in the preamble and second article, the purposes of the law are set forth, which are to strengthen the union of the cantons, to maintain and increase the unity, power, and honor of the Swiss nation, to insure the independence of the country against dangers from without, to preserve internal tranquillity and order, to protect the liberty and rights of the members, and to increase their common prosperity. This statement of aim may be compared with that contained in the Constitution of the United States, which is ordained "in order to form a more perfect union, establish justice, insure domestic tranquillity, provide for the common defense, promote the general welfare, and secure the blessings of liberty to ourselves and our posterity."[1]

Since the Swiss constitution is the fundamental law of the state, its makers are recognized as the legal sovereign in Switzerland. This sovereign, then, consists of a body embracing a majority of the voters so distributed as to make a majority in at least twelve of the cantons; for by such a body both the constitution of 1848 and the amendments of 1874 were adopted, and by a like body the present constitution may at any time be amended or revised. And the revision shall be effected by the means provided for federal legislation. Whenever one house of the federal legislature decrees the revision of the constitution, and the other house does not consent, or, indeed, whenever fifty thousand Swiss citizens having the right to vote demand the revision, a vote of the Swiss people shall be called to determine whether the constitution shall be revised or not. If in either of the cases thus submitted to popular vote, the majority of the citizens voting shall decide affirmatively, the two

[1] These clauses appear to have been transferred to the constitution of the Argentine Republic, where they occur in the preamble, in the following words: "Con el objeto de constituir la union nacional, *afianzar la justicia, consolidar la paz interior, proveer á la defensa comun, promover el bienestar jeneral, i asegurar los beneficios de la libertad para nosotros, para nuestra posteridad*, i para todos los hombres del mundo que quieran habitar el suelo argentino."

houses of the legislature shall be constituted anew to undertake the revision. The constitution having been revised in this manner by the legislative bodies, a second vote of the people is demanded for its acceptance. Accordingly, Article 121 provides that "the revised federal constitution becomes in force whenever it has been accepted by the majority of the Swiss citizens taking part in the voting, and by the majority of the cantons." The result of the popular vote in this matter is considered the vote of the canton, and the decision of the half canton is counted as a half vote.

While the Swiss constitution was adopted and may be amended by the direct vote of the people, the constitution of the United States acquired validity through its adoption by conventions of nine of the thirteen States. The direct vote of the people was not required for its adoption, nor is such a vote required for its amendment. According to Article V, "the Congress, whenever two-thirds of both Houses shall deem it necessary, shall propose amendments to this constitution, or, on the application of the legislatures of two-thirds of the several States, shall call a convention for proposing amendments, which, in either case, shall be valid to all intents and purposes as part of this Constitution, when ratified by the legislatures of three-fourths of the several States, or by conventions in three-fourths thereof, as the one or the other mode of ratification may be proposed by the Congress." The alternative method here provided is wanting in the constitution of Mexico, where, in order to effect a change, it is rerequired that the Congress of the Union, by a vote of two-thirds of the members present, agree to reforms or additions, and that these be approved by the majority of the legislatures of the States.[1] In both of these instances, as in the cases of Colombia,[2] Venezuela,[3] and the Ar-

[1] Constitucion de los Estados Unidos Mejicanos, Art. 127.

[2] Article 92 of the constitution of the Republic of Colombia contains the following provisions relative to amendment:—

"Esta constitucion podrá ser reformada total ó parcialmente con las formalidades siguientes:

"1. Que la reforma sea solicitada por la mayoría de las lejislaturas de los estados;

"2. Que la reforma sea discutida i aprobada en ámbas cámaras conforme á lo establecido para la espedicion de las leyes; i

"3. Que la reforma sea ratificada por el voto unánime del senado de plenipotenciarios, teniendo un voto cada estado.

"Tambien puede ser reformada por una convencion convocada al efecto por el congreso, á solicitud de la totalidad de las lejislaturas de los estados, i compuesta de igual número de diputados por cada estado."

[3] The amendment of the constitution of Venezuela is provided for in the following terms of Article 122:—

"Esta constitucion podrá ser reformada total ó parcialmente por la lejislatura nacional, si lo solicitare la mayoria de las lejislaturas de los estados; pero nunca se hará la reforma sino sobre los puntos á que se refieran las solicitudes de los estados."

gentine Republic,[1] the will of the people expresses itself through the fundamental law only indirectly. In Switzerland, the voters are constituent elements of the legal sovereign, while in the other cases the legal sovereign is made up of organizations of representatives or delegates who have received their authority from the voters. That body in a state is legally sovereign in which is vested the power to make or amend the fundamental law of the state; but "that body is 'politically' sovereign or supreme in a state the will of which is ultimately obeyed by the citizens of the state. In this sense of the word the electors of Great Britain may be said to be, together with the Crown and the Lords, or, perhaps, in strict accuracy, independently of the King and the Peers, the body in which sovereign power is vested. For, as things now stand, the will of the electorate and certainly of the electorate in combination with the Lords and the Crown, is sure ultimately to prevail on all subjects to be determined by the British Government."[2] "But the legally sovereign power is assuredly, as maintained by all the

[1] In the Argentine Republic, according to Article 30, "La constitucion puede reformarse en el todo ó en cualquiera de sus partes. La necesidad de reforma debe ser declarada por el congreso con el voto de dos terceras partes, al menos, de sus miembros, pero no se efectuará sino por una convencion convocada al efecto."

[2] Dicey, "The Law of the Constitution," 66–67.

best writers on the constitution, nothing but Parliament."[1] If we adopt the line of distinction here drawn by Professor Dicey, the legal sovereign in Switzerland appears to be identical with that body which is politically sovereign, while in the United States and the other federal states mentioned, these two bodies are distinct.

Inasmuch as the sovereign of a federal state requires much time for action, and can act only at considerable intervals, it is necessary that there should exist efficient agents, receiving authority from the sovereign, for the performance of specified parts of the business of government. In such a state, the larger part of the powers of the sovereign are distributed, subject always to recall, by the sovereign itself to three governmental departments, which hold in relation to the sovereign the position of agents. The sovereign is here conceived of as the holder of the absolute power of a nation, which it delegates to subordinates of its own creation or of its adoption; and every nation possesses such a power. "It may have any organization, from the purest democracy to the most absolute monarchy; but considered in its relations to the rest of mankind and to its own individual members, it must exist, to the extent at least of enacting laws for itself, as an integral, independent, sovereign

[1] Dicey, 69.

society among the other similar nations of the earth. Its government, or, in other words, the permanent agents which it has established to make efficient its organic will, must be so far independent that no other power may authoritatively control its legislation, no other state may interfere, and, according to any received and admitted constitution of things, prescribe what the laws shall be."[1] In a nation with a federal form of government, the three departments of the central organization already mentioned are not the only factors that may be viewed as agents of the sovereign power. The various offices, organizations, or institutions for exercising power in the subordinate political societies, may also be regarded as the sovereign's organs or agents; for if not created by the sovereign, the sovereign has accepted them, acts through them, and preserves their existence. The distribution of power on which much stress has been laid since Montesquieu's celebrated utterance,[2] has a larger meaning than that which has usually been ascribed to it. It involves the idea of a nation possessing, in itself an inherent, an absolute, power of self-direction, giving over to specific departments, or special classes, or subordinate organizations, or allowing to remain in subordinate bodies, such portions of this power as may

[1] Pomeroy, "Constitutional Law," 30.
[2] "De L' Esprit des Lois," L. II, ch. VI.

be consistent with its free determination. It involves not only such an allotment of power, but also the relation of State to federal authority. In a word, wherever in a nation political power exists and is exercised, except in the case of the direct action of the sovereign, it exists and is exercised as a virtual emanation from the sovereign.

An important difference between a simple democracy, like Uri or Appenzell, and a vast and complex nation, like England, the United States, or the German Empire, lies in the lack of distribution of the sovereign power in the one case and the extensive distribution necessitated by the physical conditions of the other.

In the case of the great nation, however, as the physical obstacles are overcome, there appears to be a tendency to return to the ideal of primitive democracy, in other words, for the political sovereign to crowd itself as near as possible to the current business of government. Viewed with respect to the distribution of power, the present position of England's central government suggests that, after a long series of experiments, the nation has returned almost to its point of departure. The primitive government of the existing English stock in England was the government of an isolated community, in which the whole power, as is the case to-day in some of the democratic cantons of Switzerland, rested in the hands of the freemen, and was exercised immediately by the whole body itself, or by its directly appointed agents. This was a form of government adapted only to the limited area of the primitive settlement. When these primary groups became united, and the area of the enlarged dominion became so great as to prevent the whole body of freemen from participating directly in the affairs of the state, the first step was taken towards setting up the rule of an aristocracy presided over by a king. Immediately after the union of the petty kingdoms of Anglo-Saxon England into the kingdom of Ecgberht, the popular element of the nation did not participate in the affairs of the central government. The circumstances of expanded dominion had relegated the activity of the great mass of the people to local concerns. The conditions were, therefore, favorable to the existence of an aristocratic government; and that the aristocracy which governed the English people between the tenth and thirteenth centuries was something more than an aristocracy of wealth or of birth, is sufficiently indicated by the name of the assembly through which its power was exercised. This was England's experiment with a pure aristocracy; and the ease with which it was maintained at this time was due principally to two causes: First, the ignorance of all but the few; second, the absence of any tried and approved means by which the great body of the people could put forth their power while scattered over all England. The discovery and application of means by which the power of the people could be exerted under these conditions closed the period of aristocratic exclusiveness in English politics. There followed a new experiment in the distribution of power.

The admission of city and county representatives to Parliament, in the thirteenth century, was an invasion of the aristocratic monopoly in government, and was a step towards the introduction of the democratic element to cooperation with the aristocracy. The immediate departure from aristocracy was, however, very slight, inasmuch as the counties in the beginning could be represented only by members of the nobility, and the representatives of the cities were elected by exclusive corporations. But even this slight concession was followed by a reaction in the form of the disfranchising statute of 1430. From this time onward the political history of England shows movement along several lines: First, to increase the functions of the central government at the expense of the local organizations; second, to increase, in the central

5

government itself, the power of the lower house at the expense of the Crown and the Lords; third, to make the lower house the creature of a larger and larger number of voters, and to bring the voters into an ever enlarging knowledge of, and a more immediate participation in, the current affairs of the government. These changes have resulted already in making the ministry merely a committee of the lower house, and the lower house a committee of the enfranchised part of the population.

The connection between the English ministry of to-day and the great national party which it represents is scarcely less immediate than that which existed between the original Saxon settlers and their elected officers. The Crown and Lords still exist, but an independent decision on the part of either is no longer to be thought of. Under the constitution, the Crown is endowed with the power of an absolute veto, but its exercise at present would be regarded as a revolution, so completely has custom superseded the law of two centuries ago. And the House of Lords has, under the same constitution, the power to reject any measure passed by the Commons. But no sooner is there manifest, on the part of the Lords, a disposition to exercise this power, than the nation begins to bestir itself to coerce them to conform their action to the will of the dominant party. The forms of these institutions still continue, but their ancient power has drifted back to the freemen, who exercise it in the most direct manner consistent with their large numbers. The action of the ministry must conform to the will of the majority of the Commons, and the majority of the Commons must be in accord with the majority of the electors. In this necessary harmony of the governmental executive and the bulk of the electors, is the ground for the statement that after several centuries of experiments in the matter of the distribution of power, the English people have returned to a position not essentially different from that from which they set out.

If we attempt to explain this drift of political power in England, we shall find an important cause of it in the difficulty—perhaps in the impossibility—of so distributing this power that the several departments of the government shall be held in a just and even balance. If this balance is disturbed by one department receiving more power than is necessary to place it in equilibrium with the other departments, this one department is thus enabled to encroach on the others, and, in the course of time, to dominate in the government. The power to loosen or tighten the national purse-strings was the specially efficient possession of the Commons, and constituted the principal advantage over the other departments, which have finally succumbed to its supremacy.

If the political drift which we have observed in England has an efficient cause in an inevitably unequal distribution of power, we must look for a similar tendency, or a tendency to the supremacy of some one department, whenever an attempt is made to distribute the power which is vested in the sovereign of the nation. Assuming the permanence of the fundamental principles of human nature, and the continuance of the dominant social tendencies which are revealed in history, the course of England's political progress appears as the type of the necessary evolution of popular government. This gradual drift of power towards some given point in the organism is illustrated by the history of federal governments. Even the brief history of the United States shows this tendency of power in the relation of the States to the federal government. It was supposed by the makers of the federal Constitution that they had so distributed the political power of the nation between the State and federal governments that there would be no encroachment of the one on the other. But, by placing the power of final interpretation in one of the organs of the federal government, as it was necessary to do in order that the Federation might be held together, conditions were established favorable to the gravitation of power toward the center; for the human quality of the government made it more than probable that, in cases of doubt, the interpretation would be always in its own favor. For this and other reasons, wherever in the history of the world we find a federation having an internal organization sufficiently strong to maintain its own existence, we observe an inevitable drift of power from the several States to the central government. This is true of all the federations, from the Achaian League to the United States, that have been sufficiently permanent to win a place in history. Each of these governments shows the failure of an attempt to distribute the national power in such a manner as to preserve the State and federal governments in equilibrium.

The specific movement of power which has been observed in the history of the English government, is manifest also within the central government of the United States. There is to be noted, however, this difference: in England, the absence of a written constitution, and the fact that the national legislature has been the legal sovereign, have permitted this body, without an appeal to any higher authority, to modify the government, or to shift the preponderence of power from one department or institution to another; while in the United States, similar changes have been brought about, and under the continued operation of existing forces, will hereafter be brought about, through judicial stretching and twisting of a written constitution, or through amendments of the constitution itself. The presence of a written constitution only renders slower the movement toward the accumulation of power at a single point in the governmental organization.

If we find in England alone the culmination of the tendency to bring the affairs of government into the immediate control of the electors, it must be remembered that in England alone there have been six hundred years of popular rule. In other states with popular rule, whether with restricted or universal suffrage, in which representatives of the people have the right to initiate laws, and consequently the power to shape the governmental policy, there are present the conditions and internal forces which conduce to the attainment of the same end. There appears to be wanting only time to enable all popular governments to reach essentially the same position, politically, that England has already reached, or that position in which the English will find themselves on the attainment of universal suffrage. All·the dominant forces of existing Aryan society, those derived from the spread of popular education, from the increasing intercourse between communities and classes, and from the growing recognition of political equality, contribute to the establishment of this tendency. It finds confirmation, moreover, in the history and organization of popular governments everywhere. Our national history shows that in the United States there has been a marked drift of power towards the central government, and in the central government itself, a drift of power towards the lower house. In short, every representative government in which the representatives of the people have the right to initiate laws, however the political power of the nation may have been distributed at first, tends to move in a certain course, whose end, or culmination, is the nearest practicable connection between the voters of the dominant national party and the actual business of government. When this point is reached, and the whole burden of governing a great nation rests, as in England, on a committee of the representatives of the people, the political cycle of that nation is run. And when it is found, as it has been found in England, that the business devolving upon the governing committee is so multifarious and complex as to render its proper execution impossible, the time has arrived for a redistribution of power.

After the passage of one more reform bill, making the suffrage universal, this will be essentially the position of England. In view of the fact that the political power formerly possessed by the Crown and the Lords has been transferred to the Commons, and that the Commons have become the creatures of the whole enfranchised part of the nation, and the electors are thus brought as near as practicable to the actual conduct of affairs, there remains no important step to be taken in this direction.

The tendency of centuries having found here its culmination, there are abundant reasons for supposing that the next important change in English political life will be the result of a great reconstructive effort, put forth to create new and efficient organs of power in place of the Crown and the Lords; or, more particularly, in place of the Lords, whose functions, aside from their activity in behalf of their own perpetuation, have dwindled to merely those of opposition, yet an opposition which may always be overcome in the last resort.

At this point—that is, at the culmination of this tendency to bring the electors into the closest possible proximity to governmental affairs—it is asserted that there must be a redistribution of power. The reasons for this assertion may not be exhaustively given. It may, however, be said in general that the attainment of rational freedom is one of the chief ends of the state, and that it is only through the means of political institutions that this end may be attained. If, therefore, the tendency which we have considered is to break down and ignore these institutions, it is clear that they must be revived, or new ones created, before the state can be in a position to secure its legitimate purpose; and the revival or creation of political institutions is simply another phrase for the distribution or redistribution of political power. It may be stated, moreover, as a general principle of social activity, that there is a tendency in society to put forth its efforts for self-conservation and progress, in the line of least resistance; and it follows from this that no institutions which have lost all their functions but those of obstruction, can permanently remain a part of the social organism. They will ultimately either be supplanted by others, or be once more endowed with the power of positive action; and to effect either of these results there will be necessary a redistribution of that power which has drifted into the hands of the people. If at this point such redistribution does not take place, we have to suppose that all that activity which, since the beginning of political life, has been devoted to a fancied improvement of the form of the government, will at once and forever cease, a supposition entirely at variance with the known laws of social activity. There is another and a practical consideration which—the supposition having been reached—will urge imperatively the redistribution of power. I refer to the actual inability of the ministers, where the power of a great nation rests with them, as in England, to carry to a proper and successful issue all the varied and far-reaching undertakings that devolve upon them.

England, therefore, seems about to be called upon to face the great question of the redistribution of her political power. By this statement, it is not meant that the work must be undertaken this year or the next, but that it is a task of the future from which there appears no escape. If, moreover, present tendencies are indications of future conditions, it is a task which will ultimately present itself to every nation whose government rests for its primary foundation on the will of the people. In a federal republic, like the United States, the tendency observed in England may exist, but be checked from time to time by constitutional amendment or by decisions of the Supreme Court, thus avoiding an important redistribution at any one time. In all governments there are forces which conduce to the same end, although in some the full manifestation may be prevented by the operation of counteracting forces which redistribute the power as fast as it is aggregated. While, however, it may be readily admitted that the history of our national life shows a tendency to place more and more power in the central government, it may, perhaps, be denied that there is any evidence of power drifting away from the President and the Senate, and tending to concentrate itself in the House of Representatives. A careful examination, however, will reveal certain considerations drawn from the nature of the lower house, and from its relation to other departments of the government, that suggest its ultimate supremacy, and the gradual crowding of the people nearer and nearer to the actual exercise of power. To indicate two or three of these we may mention: 1. The relatively greater and greater importance which the finances are assuming in the affairs of legislation and administration, coupled with the fact that in these matters the lower house alone possesses the right of the initiative. 2. The claim of the lower house to be heard in the making of treaties, which is fixed by the Constitution clearly as a function of the President and the Senate.

3. The more intimate relation which members of this house hold to the great body of the people, and the greater share of popular confidence which for this reason they are likely to enjoy; or, in other words, the increasing power and prestige which, in the progress of democracy, the members of the lower house are to acquire more and more abundantly, as the bearers of the most direct, and consequently the most authoritative, message from the electors. 4. The demand of the voters that the representatives shall pledge themselves to vote as directed by their constituents.

These are a few of a very long list of facts which indicate not only the disposition of the great body of electors to lay their hands directly on the machinery of government, but also their ability to advance toward their desired end. Our political drift, then, is manifestly to bring the people nearer the actual operations of legislation and administration. The happy feature of a federal government in this connection is, that the remedy of too great an accumulation of power at any one point is found in an amendment of the constitution; and the authority to amend is so distributed as to make it antagonistic to the absorption of all power at any single point of the political organism. The question of redistribution of power in such a state is,

DISTRIBUTION OF POWER. 77

therefore, a very simple affair, but with a government like that of England it is a question of adopting a new form. It is, therefore, pertinent to inquire into the constitutional possibilities of the future; that is to say, viewing the future from the standpoint of the existing forces of society, what forms of government are likely to be accepted in the later stages of our social growth? It is, of course, to be understood that there are certain general constitutional possibilities which hold with respect to the social conditions of all Western nations, and certain particular possibilities which hold with respect only to certain particular nations. This topic is of primary importance, because it is highly desirable to know what forms of government have a chance of existing in the future, in order that, in advancing to the great question of the redistribution of power, arguments may not be wasted to show that a given form of government is the best form, when a little thoughtful observation and reflection would show that it lies clearly without the field of constitutional possibilities. It may not be easy to determine definitely the limits of this field, yet there are doubtless some things in governmental organization which the race has outgrown. If we can determine these by examining the history of governments in the light of the inherent tendencies of society, we can indicate certain forms of political organization which it is useless to advocate, and by this means indicate approximately the constitutional possibilities of the future.

There is probably no other form of government which accords so generally with the preferences of thoughtful men as aristocracy. It is easy to persuade one's self that a government of the best is the best form of government for any nation. Yet it is not altogether clear that this form of government, as generally understood and advocated, is not antiquated, and, at least as it appears in the political history of the world, no longer among those forms which should be the aim of our political striving. At any rate, two questions arise respecting it: 1. Is its record such that its continued existence is desirable? 2. Are the conditions of modern life favorable to its continuance?

If we were to pass in review the whole record of aristocratic rule, the resulting conclusion would be that wherever the power of government has rested undisturbed in the hands of an aristocratic class, this class has inclined more and more to wield this power to its own material advantage, while, at the same time, the spontaneous life of the people has been suppressed, and the intelligence of the nation crystallized into a stiff and unproductive formalism. Compare aristocratic

Sparta with the more democratic Athens, or Venice with Florence. The creative intellect has left no record of great activity under a strictly aristocratic government.

Regarding the second question, as to the prospects of any historical form of aristocracy under the conditions of modern life, there is abundant evidence that it is not likely to fit in well with the ideas and social organization of the future. Aristocracy has entered into the government of states either as the sole power, or as a power co-ordinated with a prince, or with a body representing the people, or with both. Where it appears in the second form, that is, as a power co-ordinated with another power in the government, it is the product of times whose fundamental idea as to the source of political power and privilege was totally different from that at present generally entertained. The mediæval pretension of the Pope, that he was the vicar of God on earth, charged with the control of man's spiritual interests, was the practical foundation of that theory which regarded the prince, or head of the state, as the source of all the political power exercised in the government of the nation; for if the Pope controlled man's spiritual interests, it was clear to the mediæval mind that the temporal interests, which were plainly inferior to the spiritual, should be subordinated, through the prince, to the bearer of the high commission of spiritual control. Thus, the divine right to direct the worldly concerns of a nation, to appoint officers, and to bestow privileges, descended upon the prince through God's appointed agent. Under this view, through the appointment of the prince, arose those aristocracies which, in some countries, at present divide the power with the popular element. But the great revolution of the last three hundred years has its central and essential feature in the introduction and adoption of the idea that whatever power is exercised in the government is derived, not from the head of the state, but from the bulk of the nation. This view is accepted even by nations whose affairs are administered under the fictions and precedents derived from their earlier history. The English furnish an instance of this. In theory, the revolution may be considered to be complete. No one in these days writes as Sir Robert Filmer wrote in his "Patriarcha." If, in official titles and forms of administration, we are constantly pointed to a former phase of political life, it is to be remembered that these titles and forms are only survivals of an age whose spirit has departed. With this revolution, then, disappears the head of the state as the source of aristocratic power and privilege;

at least, as the source of that form of aristocracy which is represented in the English peerage, and which, before 1866, was represented in the nobility of Sweden. For it is not to be supposed that a crown which exists only by a parliamentary title, and which has no power of independent political action, will remain permanently the source of the power of an important department of the government.

History, however, shows us another phase of aristocracy, which does not proceed from the appointment of a divinely sanctioned political head. Such an aristocracy we find in those states which have been governed by a select few, without the co-operation of a body of popular representatives. These have been chiefly small states, like the states of the Netherlands, some of the Italian Republics, many of the republics of antiquity, and a number of the cantons of Switzerland. Among the special conditions favorable to the existence of aristocratic governments in these cases were: First, the fact that only a small part of the population were really free, the majority being in Greece, slaves, and in the modern states feudal vassals; second, the absence of the system of representation, which was unknown among the ancients; third, the ignorance of the great body of the people, and their consequent inability to combine for their own advantage. But, in the course of modern progress, all these conditions have been swept away. Slavery and vassalage are gone, except as the latter appears in the allegiance of employees in great enterprises to their employers; and in place of the ignorant populace of the ancient and mediæval world, there has appeared a lower stratum of society, sufficiently educated to use the means of acquiring information, and eager to proclaim and forcibly urge their own rights, as interpreted by themselves. Aristocracy of this form having fallen by the removal of its ancient supports, it has been rendered practically impossible in the future, by the introduction of political representation, and by the spread of free public education, which acts, in the first place, as a great leveling force, and in the second place, promotes a sufficient degree of intelligence to enable the masses to perceive the advantage they may derive by employing a system of political representation. Aristocracy, then, in either of its historical forms, may be set down as practically outside of the constitutional possibilities of the time towards which we are drifting.

These and other considerations lead to the conclusion that in the future distribution of power in England, in spite of the English love of aristocracy, the aristocratic element, as such, will disappear from the government, as it has already disappeared from the governments of certain other nations. On this point the case of Sweden is significant, because Sweden and England have followed essentially the same course of political development, the main difference being that class distinctions have been more sharply drawn in Sweden than in England. In England the representatives of the counties and of the cities were united in a single assembly—the House of Commons—but in Sweden each of these two classes of representatives constituted an assembly by itself. In England the nobles and the clergy joined to form the upper house; but in Sweden these classes met separately, and constituted the third and fourth houses of the Swedish Parliament. In the Swedish parliamentary reform of 1866, the aristocratic element was set aside, and the national legislature was made to consist of two elective houses, the lower formed by a direct, the upper by an indirect, election.

If there are reasons which point to the disappearance of aristocracy from the governments to which our descendants will pay allegiance, particularly our English descendants, there are still stronger reasons for regarding absolute monarchy, of the Bourbon type, entirely and forever antiquated. The only form of monarchy which the dominant forces of modern political society do not controvert, is that which, like the Napoleonic monarchy, has its constitutive in the suffrages of the nation. And in one view this form of monarchy appears as the legitimate outcome, or ultimate phase, of popular government. However the power in a republic may be distributed, however numerous the checks and balances set up, the results of the governmental activity will never exactly accord with the wishes and expectations of the great body of the electors. It may be a very fortunate circumstance in the long run that this is so; nevertheless, the fact remains, and comes back to the minds of the voters with ever renewed force, that they are living under a government nominally directed by themselves, of whose results they have every day reason to complain. They feel that something is wrong, and in view of this there arises distrust of those in office. Somebody must have betrayed a trust, or everything would be right. Restricting the officers to specific instructions is found to be impracticable. From the difficulties of the situation there is, to the muddled mind of the voter, no surer means of escape than to fix upon one man of supreme ability and heavenly intentions, and to give him all power, but make him responsible to the voters. Thus arises the imperial government which appears to have yet a rôle to play in the world.

If the experience and historical tendencies of the Aryan race go for anything, our descendants will confine their allegiance to variations of two forms of government: the representative republic and a monarchy constituted by popular suffrage. The former will almost necessarily obtain in nations where skill in local self-government has been acquired and maintained in practice. On the other hand, a nation wanting in the traditions and practice of local self-government will be liable to frequent changes from one form to the other. In France, where certain officers of local government are appointed by the central authority, it is a matter of little moment to the great body of the people whether the central government is republican or imperial. The people of New England, however, knowing that a transition from republican to imperial rule would involve the substitution of officers appointed by a central government for their own elected local officers, would not hasten to make the change. The force of the tradition of local self-government in England, and the continuing power of existing local organizations, make it practically necessary for the English, in the work of redistributing their political power, to leave the Napoleonic form of monarchy entirely out of consideration. They, therefore, appear to be limited to some form of a representative republic as the outcome of their reconstructive efforts; and not unlikely the federal form will be found best adapted to the somewhat heterogeneous character of the present British Empire.

Under the impression which the recent "blood and iron" policy of Prussia has made in the world, it may perhaps be objected that, although Germany has representative institutions, and even universal suffrage, it does not show that drift of power which we have observed particularly in England and in the United States. The objection, however, arises from an imperfect understanding of the spirit of German history. As it regards the government, the history of Germany is divided into two parts by the Napoleonic wars. Between the middle of the tenth century and the early part of the nineteenth, Germany was a great feudal empire. It differed from the feudal kingdom of France in the slowness of its development, and in the weakness and final failure of the central power. The feudal bond was not completely broken in Germany until 1806, when Francis II. was compelled to lay down the imperial crown. This was the end of one phase of German history. With respect to the imperial government, this phase is marked by a gradual dissolution. The Congress of Vienna, at the close of the Napoleonic wars, opens the constructive period.

The German States at this time were without any legal bond of union. The work to be done was to take these fragments, each endowed with sovereign power, and mould them into a nation. Since the Congress of Vienna the Germans have been laboring in this undertaking, sometimes with feeble and misguided efforts, sometimes with the mightiest exhibitions of political skill and military force that the world has ever seen. The events of the last seventy years of German history become intelligible only when viewed as steps towards founding a national state. The Germanic Confederation, formed at Vienna to be under the presidency of Austria, was too loose to furnish an efficient central government. It failed, moreover, because it embraced two great powers with incompatible aims. The efforts of 1848–49 were a second attempt at national unity. The failure of this attempt made it clear that a new method must be tried. It was idle to expect all the powers to unite at once. Those of one mind were united in the North German Confederation, which in 1870 had been extended so as to embrace all the German States but Austria. The next year the North German Confederation was transformed into the German Empire. Through the federal constitution of the empire, the way is at last open to a strong national government.

88   GOVERNMENT OF SWITZERLAND.

Some reasons for this statement are: First, the fact that the constitution cannot be changed without the consent of Prussia, taken in connection with the fact that it is for the interest of Prussia to have only such changes made as will strengthen the imperial government, as compared with the State governments; second, the manifest drift of power towards the center, during the eighteen years of imperial rule; in a word, the inevitable growth in a federation, when the central government is made strong enough to command the local governments. If, now, the imperial government is to maintain itself, and become in time more thoroughly centralized, it is clear that the Bundesrath, which is composed of ambassadors from the several States, must decline in importance as compared with the Reichstag, which is constituted by universal suffrage. The more centralized the empire becomes, the more immediate becomes the emperor's dealing with the Reichstag; and, under these circumstances, all the forces that have operated in England to magnify the Commons will operate here, in a greater or less degree, to magnify the Reichstag. Wherefore, although a position similar to that which England has reached may be a long way off for the Germans, it is, nevertheless, the necessary outcome for a government which places in the hands of a popular assembly like the Reichstag matters of such vital importance as the national revenues and expenditures. We shall read, therefore, in the history of the German Empire not a new revelation, but a new illustration of the old doctrine of the distribution of political power.

In a federal government this question is more complicated than elsewhere, for it involves not only the relation of department to department, but also the relation sustained by the central to the local government. This relation in all conspicuous federal states, except Canada, is essentially that set forth in the tenth amendment of the United States Constitution, namely, that the powers not delegated to the general government "by the Constitution, nor prohibited by it to the States, are reserved to the States respectively, or to the people." But in Canada the opposite principle obtains. Article 91 of the British North America Act affirms that "it shall be lawful for the queen, by and with the advice and consent of the Senate and House of Commons, to make laws for the peace, order, and good government of Canada in relation to all matters not coming within the classes of subjects by this act assigned exclusively to the legislatures of the provinces." The classes of subjects thus assigned are enumerated in Article 92, and are as follows:—

"1. The amendment from time to time, notwithstanding anything in this act, of the constitution of the province, except as regards the office of lieutenant-governor.

"2. Direct taxation within the province in order to the raising of a revenue for provincial purposes.

"3. The borrowing of money on the sole credit of the province.

"4. The establishment and tenure of provincial offices, and the appointment and payment of provincial officers.

"5. The management and sale of the public lands belonging to the province, and of the timber and wood thereon.

"6. The establishment, maintenance, and management of public and reformatory prisons in and for the province.

"7. The establishment, maintenance, and management of hospitals, asylums, charities, and eleemosynary institutions in and for the province, other than marine hospitals.

"8. Municipal institutions in the province.

"9. Shop, saloon, tavern, and auctioneer, and other licenses, in order to the raising of a revenue for provincial, local, or municipal purposes.

"10. Local works and undertakings, other than such as are of the following classes:—

"*a.* Lines of steam or other ships, railways,

canals, telegraphs, and other works and undertakings connecting the province with any other or others of the provinces, or extending beyond the limits of the province.

"*b.* Lines of steamships between the province and any British or foreign country.

"*c.* Such works as, although wholly situate within the province, are before or after their execution declared by the parliament of Canada to be for the general advantage of Canada or for the advantage of two or more of the provinces.

"11. The incorporation of companies with provincial objects.

"12. Solemnization of marriage in the province.

"13. Property and civil rights in the province.

"14. The administration of justice in the province, including the constitution, maintenance, and organization of provincial courts, both of civil and of criminal jurisdiction, and including procedure in civil matters in those courts.

"15. The imposition of punishment by fine, penalty, or imprisonment for enforcing any law of the province made in relation to any matter coming within any of the classes of subjects enumerated in this section.

"16. Generally all matters of a merely local or private nature in the province."

Through this departure from the general practice of federations the Dominion has "avoided," according to Sir J. A. Macdonald, "the great source of weakness which has been the cause of the disruption of the United States." The essential point of this opinion still finds supporters. "In arranging this part of the constitution," says Dr. Bourinot, "its framers had before them the experience of eighty years' working of the federal system of the United States, and were able to judge in what essential and fundamental respects that system appeared to be defective. The doctrine of State sovereignty had been pressed to extreme lengths in the United States, and had formed one of the most powerful arguments of the advocates of secession. This doctrine had its origin in the fact that all powers, not expressly conferred upon the general government, are reserved in the constitution to the States. Now in the federal constitution of Canada the very reverse principle obtains, with the avowed object of strengthening the basis of the confederation, and preventing conflict as far as practicable between the provinces that compose the Union."[1]

It is to be observed that in forming the tenth amendment of the United States Constitution, the word *expressly*, which appears in the second

[1] Bourinot, "Parliamentary Procedure and Practice," 81.

article of the Articles of Confederation, was omitted, thus leaving the general government greater freedom than it would otherwise have had in exercising implied powers. In Mexico,[1] Colombia,[2] Venezuela,[3] and the Argentine Republic,[4] the field for the discretionary exercise of implied powers is more strictly limited than in the United States; for whatever power is exercised by the federal organization in each of these cases, must be expressly, or, as the constitution of Colombia provides, "expressly, specially, and clearly" delegated to it.[5] In each of these cases, moreover, the powers of the congress are enumerated in a series of clauses after the manner observed in the Constitution of the United States; and in some instances the language employed is evidently a direct translation of the words of the model.

The scope of the German imperial government is limited to the exercise of powers delegated to it, and is sufficiently indicated by an enumeration of the subjects that have been turned over to its control. They may be set down under the following heads:—

[1] Constitution of Mexico, Art. 117.
[2] Constitution of Colombia, Art. 16.
[3] Constitution of Venezuela, Art. 90.
[4] Constitution of the Argentine Republic, Art. 104.
[5] "Todos los asuntos de gobierno, cuyo ejercicio no deleguen los estados *espresa, especial i claramente* al gobierno jeneral, son de la esclusiva competencia de los mismos estados." Art. 16.

1. The administration of the imperial finances, especially the customs duties, the imperial taxes, and the emission of funded and unfunded paper money.

2. Foreign affairs, together with the protection of German trade in foreign countries, and of navigation on the high seas.

3. The imperial army and navy.

4. The civil law, criminal law, and judicial procedure; the protection of copyright; provisions for the authorization of public documents, and decisions regarding denial of justice.

5. Surveillance of foreigners and issuing and examining passports.

6. The press and associations.

7. The surveillance of the medical and veterinary professions.

8. The principles governing the rights of emigration, the poor laws, and laws referring to residence and colonization.

9. Legislation relation to trade and industry, including insurance and banking; weights, measures, and coinage, and patents for inventions.

10. Railway matters, and the construction of means of communication by land and water for the purposes of home defense and of general commerce. Rafting and navigation on those waters which are common to several States, and the condition of such waters, as likewise river and other water dues; also navigation signals.

11. Postal and telegraphic affairs.

The competence of the empire with respect to these matters was subject to certain limitations: "1. Hamburg and Bremen, for the time being, were excluded from the tariff legislation, as free ports. 2. In Bavaria, Würtemberg, and Baden, the beer and brandy tax was reserved for the special legislation of these States; and the same was true of the beer tax in the province of Alsace-Lorraine. 3. Bavaria and Würtemberg manage independently their postal and telegraphic affairs in accordance with certain principles established by imperial legislation. 4. Both States enjoy, with respect to military affairs, certain exceptional rights. 5. With reference to Bavaria, the legislation relating to residence and colonization has no application, as that relating to railways has only a limited application."[1]

The doctrine of the Swiss constitution on this point is that the cantons are sovereign in so far as their sovereignty is not limited by the federal constitution, and, as such, they exercise all the rights which are not delegated to the federal power.[2] In the Act of Mediation and in the drafts of 1832 and 1833, it was required that the general government should exercise only such powers as were *expressly* delegated, as was the

[1] De Grais, "Handbuch der Verfassung und Verwaltung in Preussen und dem deutschen Reiche." 11-13.
[2] Article 3.

case under the Articles of Confederation in America. But in forming the constitution of 1848, the word *"expressément"* was omitted, just as the corresponding word had been omitted in forming the present Constitution of the United States, and with respect to this point the rule of these two constitutions is the same. The power of the general government of Switzerland, like that of the United States, "extends not merely to those affairs which are turned over to it by the exact words of the constitution itself, but also to the relations whose control by the central government appears as a necessity for its performance of the duties devolving upon it."[1]

[1] Blumer, I, 178.

CHAPTER IV.

THE LEGISLATURE.

OF the several governmental departments in a federal state, the legislative is the most conspicuous, although co-ordinate with the executive and judicial departments, and deriving its authority from a source of power common to all. In the federal state, "there are not only organized individual States but also a completely organized central and common state,"[1] and the legislature of the central and common state is so constituted as to take account of the whole body of the people who make up the nation, and of the individual States within the larger or-

---

[1] Bluntschli, "Geschichte des schw. Bundesrechtes." I, 562. The distinctive characteristics of a federal government, as indicated by Arosemena, are: (1) "That the entities now united may have had an individual life previously, which they preserve while they delegate to a government general and common the functions which are necessary to constitute nationality; (2) that the sectional government be maintained independent of the national and common government, both in its formation and in its development." "Estudios Constitucionales," I, 199.

ganism. Although the citizens of the whole nation are represented in the lower house, yet they are represented not as one body, but as several individual groups whose geographical limits are the limits of the several States. When it is provided that there shall be one representative for every fifty thousand inhabitants, and for each fraction of this number not less than twenty thousand, as in Colombia, or for each twenty-five thousand and fraction of at least twelve thousand, as in Venezuela, or for each twenty thousand and fraction of at least ten thousand, as in the Argentine Republic and Switzerland, or for each forty thousand and each fraction of at least twenty thousand, as in Mexico, or for each one hundred thousand and fraction of at least fifty thousand, as in the German Empire, the number to be divided by the number required for each representative is the number of the inhabitants of each of the several States, and the fraction is the remainder after such division.[1] Thus the

[1] Under the Constitution of the United States "the number of Representatives shall not exceed one for every thirty thousand, but each State shall have at least one Representative." Awaiting the first enumeration of the inhabitants, which was required to be made "within three years after the first meeting of the Congress," an apportionment of the Representatives to be elected was made among the several States in such a manner that New Hampshire was entitled to choose three, Massachusetts eight, Rhode Island and Providence Plantations one, Connecticut five, New York six, New Jersey four, Pennsylvania

individuality of the States is not set aside even in the organization of that legislative body which stands as the direct representative of the people.

The conditions of the suffrage under which the members of the lower house are elected in the several countries already considered, are (1) determined in a general way by the federal constitution, leaving details to be fixed by law, as in Switzerland, Canada, and the German Empire, or (2) left by that instrument to be determined by federal legislation, as in Mexico and the Argentine Republic, or (3) left to the free determination of the several States, as in Colombia, Venezuela, and the United States. Under the Swiss constitution, elections for members of the lower house are direct, and are held in federal districts that are subdivisions of the cantons.

eight, Delaware one, Maryland six, Virginia ten, North Carolina five, South Carolina five, and Georgia three (Art. I, Sec. 2). The ratio of representation in the House of Representatives has, however, been changed with each successive census, except the second, as shown by the following tabular account:—

From 1789 to 1792 according to Constitution..... 30,000
" 1792 to 1803 based on 1st Census 1790..... 33,000
" 1803 to 1812 " 2d " 1800..... 33,000
" 1812 to 1823 " 3d " 1810..... 35,000
" 1823 to 1832 " 4th " 1820 40,000
" 1832 to 1843 " 5th " 1830..... 47,700
" 1843 to 1852 " 6th " 1840..... 70,680
" 1852 to 1863 " 7th " 1850..... 93,423
" 1863 to 1872 " 8th " 1860.....127,381
" 1872 to 1882 " 9th " 1870.....131,425
" 1882 to " 10th " 1880.....154,325

Every male Swiss twenty years of age who has not been deprived of the right of active citizenship by the canton in which he resides, has the right to vote. Nevertheless, the federal legislature may regulate in a uniform manner the exercise of this right. Any layman having the right to vote is eligible to membership in this house.

In the British North America Act it was provided that "until the Parliament of Canada otherwise provides, all laws in force in the several provinces at the union relative to the following matters or any of them, namely,— the qualifications and disqualifications of persons to be elected or to sit or vote as members of the House of Assembly or Legislative Assembly in the several provinces, the voters at elections of such members, the oaths to be taken by voters, the returning officers, their powers and duties, the proceedings at elections, the periods during which elections may be continued, the trial of controverted elections, and proceedings incident thereto, the vacating of seats of members, and the execution of new writs, in case of seats vacated otherwise than by dissolution—shall respectively apply to elections of members to serve in the House of Commons for the same several provinces."[1] But at present the elections to the House of Com-

[1] Article 41.

mons are carried on under the provisions of the Dominion Elections Act, 1874, as amended by the acts of 1878 and 1882, and of the Electoral Franchise Acts of 1885 and 1886,[1] the provincial regulations temporarily adopted by the British North America Act being thus superseded by this subsequent legislation. Voters under the existing law must be British subjects by birth or naturalization, twenty-one years of age, and have a certain property qualification.

According to the constitution of the German Empire, "the members of the Reichstag shall be elected by universal suffrage, and by direct secret ballot,"[2] and until further legislation the electoral law for the Reichstag of the North German Union, of May 31, 1869, was accepted as the electoral law of the empire. By this law the voter must be at least twenty-five years old, in the full enjoyment of civil rights, and, at the time of voting, not in the service of the army or navy.[3]

In Mexico, citizenship belongs to those who are Mexicans either by birth or naturalization, and who have completed their eighteenth year

[1] Pope, "Dominion Elections Act, 1874," etc., Ottawa, 1887.

[2] Translations of this constitution and of this law are printed in papers relating to Foreign Relations of the United States, transmitted to Congress, with the Annual Message of the President, 1877, pp. 210, 212.

[3] Article 20.

of age, if married, or their twenty-first year, if unmarried, and who have an honorable means of obtaining a livelihood. Among the prerogatives of citizenship enumerated by the constitution are the privileges of voting at the popular elections and of being voted for for all elective offices, and of being appointed to any other employment or commission, provided the qualifications established by law for such office, employment, or commission have been met.[1] By the vote of Mexican citizens who have fulfilled these conditions the Chamber of Deputies is constituted; and, in accordance with Article 55, "the election of deputies shall be indirect in the first degree, by a closed ballot, under conditions prescribed by the electoral law." The States are divided into electoral districts of forty thousand inhabitants each, the fraction of at least twenty thousand electing a deputy, like a complete district; but in case the fraction is less than this number, the electors are added to the district whose capi-

[1] Art. 34. Son ciudadanos de la república todos los que, teniendo la calidad de mejicanos, reunan además las siguientes:

1. Haber cumplido diez i ocho años siendo casados, ó veintiuno si no lo son;

2. Tener un modo honesto de vivir.

Art. 35. Son prerogativas del ciudadono:

1. Votar en las elecciones populares;

2. Poder ser votado para todos los cargos de eleccion popular, i nombrado para cualquier otro empleo ó comision, teniendo las calidades que la lei establezca.

THE LEGISLATURE. 103

tal is nearest. The municipalities of the districts are divided into sections of five hundred inhabitants, each one of which elects an elector. The electors of the several sections form an electoral college, which meets in the capital or the respective district. This electoral body then elects one deputy, votes for a president of the Republic, for the members of the supreme court and four supernumeraries, and for an attorney-general. The candidate for deputy who receives an absolute majority of the votes of the college is elected; but if no one receive such a majority on the first ballot, a second ballot is taken on the two who have received the relative majority.

While in Mexico the members of the lower house are elected by an indirect vote, one member from each of the electoral districts into which the States are divided, in the Argentine Republic they are "elected directly by the people of the provinces and of the capital, which for this purpose are considered as electoral districts of a single state, and by a simple plurality of votes." The representative, however, must be twenty-five years old, have been four years a citizen, and have been born in the province which elects him, or have resided in it for two years immediately preceding the election. The constitutions of Colombia and Venezuela assert in almost the same words that "it belongs to the States to determine the manner of making the appointment of senators and representatives," thus leaving the matter wholly in the hands of the law-making power of the several States.[1] Under the Constitution of the United States, the power of the individual State in this regard is somewhat more restricted, inasmuch as the State is debarred from imposing upon voters for congressmen any conditions or qualifications different from those "requisite for electors of the most numerous branch of the State legislature."[2] It is still further restricted by the fifteenth amendment to the Constitution, which provides that "the right of citizens of the United States to vote shall not be denied or abridged by the United States or by any State on account of race, color, or previous condition of servitude." But, aside from these restrictions, the power of the State is complete.

In the constitution of the upper house, or senate, of a federal state, not only are the States as political societies recognized, but generally also the organism itself in each. It is a rule

[1] Article 40 of the Constitution of Colombia is as follows: "Corresponde á los estados determinar la manera de hacer el nombramiento de sus senadores i representantes;" and Article 19 of the Constitution of Venezuela: "Los estados determinarán la manera de hacer el nombramiento de senadores i diputados."

[2] Constitution of the United States, Art. 1, Sec. 2.

moreover, but a rule with certain exceptions, that the members of the upper house receive their appointments from the governments of the subordinate States, the manner of appointment often being left to the will of the State. In Switzerland, the manner of appointment, the term of service, and the compensation are left to the determination of the canton. If in the purely democratic cantons the members of the Council of States, or Senate, are elected by the popular assemby of the canton, it may still be regarded as an appointment by the government, since the popular assembly holds essentially the same position in the governmental organization of the canton that the legislature performing the same office holds in the governmental organization of a State in the American Union. In the other cantons, the senators are elected by the Great Council. The Argentine Republic follows a rule in most respects like that observed in the United States. "The Senate is composed of two senators from each province, elected by their legislatures by a plurality of votes; and two from the capital, elected according to the form prescribed for the election of the president of the nation."[1] The Mexican constitution also provides not only for two senators from each of the States, but at the same time for two from the

[1] The Argentine Constitution, Art. 46.

federal district; and with reference to their election, it provides that "the election of senators shall be indirect in the first degree. The legislature of each State shall declare elected the person who shall have obtained the absolute majority of all the votes cast," and the electoral college which votes for the senators is the body which votes for the deputies, the president of the republic, and the members of the supreme court.

In Colombia and Venezuela, the constitution simply leaves the manner of electing or appointing the senators to the determination of the States. The members of the Federal Council of the German Empire, if we may view this body as the upper house of a federal state, are appointed by the governments of the subordinate States; they, moreover, serve these governments in the Federal Council, in the capacity of ambassadors rather than as representatives, and vote according to instructions. But in Canada, under the British North America Act, the senators are appointed by the governor-general in the queen's name, and hold their positions for life. The appointee must, however, be able to comply with the following qualifications:—

"1. He shall be of the full age of thirty years;

"2. He shall be either a natural-born subject of the queen, or a subject of the queen naturalized by an act of the parliament of Great Britain, or of the parliament of the United Kingdom of Great Britain and Ireland, or of the legislature of one of the provinces of Upper Canada, Lower Canada, Canada, Nova Scotia, or New Brunswick, before the union, or of the parliament of Canada after the union;

"3. He shall be legally or equitably seized as of freehold for his own use and benefit of lands or tenements held in free and common socage, or seized or possessed for his own use and benefit of lands or tenements held in franc-alleu or in roture, within the province for which he is appointed, of the value of four thousand dollars, over and above all rents, dues, debts, charges, mortgages, and incumbances due or payable out of, or charged on or affecting the same;

"4. His real and personal property shall be together worth four thousand dollars over and above his debts and liabilities;

"5. He shall be resident in the province for which he is appointed;

"6. In the case of Quebec, he shall have his real property qualification in the electoral division for which he is appointed, or shall be resident in that division."[1]

With these qualifications for senatorship in Canada may be compared the requirements set by the Constitution of the United States, in which

[1] The British North America Act, 1867, Art. 23.

it is provided that "no person shall be a senator who shall not have attained to the age of thirty years, and been nine years a citizen of the United States, and who shall not, when elected, be an inhabitant of that State for which he shall be chosen."[1] The constitutions of Colombia and the empire make no provisions as to the age of senators and members of the Federal Council. But in the other states under consideration, where any voter may be a senator, the age of thirty is a common requirement. Besides the requirement of age, the other qualifications for the position of senator in Mexico are the same as those specified for a member of the lower house of the federal congress. In the Argentine Republic, he must, moreover, have been six years a citizen of the nation, be in receipt of an annual income of two thousand dollars, and have been born in the province which elects him, or have resided in it for two years immediately preceding the election. In Venezuela, however, the only requisite, aside from that of age, is that he be a citizen of Venezuela by birth.

In the senates of the federal republics, the political equality of the States is recognized, each State sending two senators, except Colombia, where each State is represented in the

[1] Constitution of the United States, Art. 1, Sec. 3.

THE LEGISLATURE. 109

senate by three members. In Switzerland each half-canton elects one senator. Each of these nations in its struggle for an independent existence has associated the notion of equality with its ideal of liberty. But Canada and the German Empire have never known such a struggle, and have adhered to their monarchial prepossessions in favor of inequality. In constituting their upper houses, moreover, the political inequality of the States has been maintained. In Canada the number of senators is seventy-eight. Of these, twenty-four are for Ontario, twenty-four for Quebec, ten for Nova Scotia, ten for New Brunswick, three for Manitoba, and three for British Columbia. "In case of the admission of Newfoundland, the normal number of senators shall be seventy-six, and their maximum number shall be eighty-two."[1] The Federal Council of the German Empire comprises fifty-eight members, of whom Prussia sends seventeen, Bavaria six, Saxony and Würtemberg four each, Baden and Hesse three each, Mecklenburg-Schwerin and Brunswick two each, and each of the other States one. Although Prussia has seventeen members to Bavaria's six, yet her superiority here is not in proportion to her superiority in population; for while she has less than three times as many members as Bavaria

[1] The British North America Act, 1867, Art. 147.

in the Federal Council, she has more than five times as many inhabitants. Prussia has, moreover, less than five times as many members as Saxony, but more than nine times as many inhabitants. In a word, although the smaller States have not the same number of members in the Federal Council as the larger, yet they have a larger membership in proportion to their population. The terms for which the members of the two houses are elected in the several federations vary from two to nine years, of course not taking into account the life service of the appointed Canadian senators. In the Argentine Republic and the United States, the senators are elected for a very much longer period than the members of the lower house. In the former state, the senatorial term is nine years, while the representatives are elected for a term of four years, which may be compared with the respective terms of six and two years in the United States. But in Mexico, Switzerland, and Venezuela, the senators and representatives hold office for equal terms: two years in Mexico and Venezuela, and three years in Switzerland. Three years is also the term of election for the Reichstag, but the members of the Federal Council serve according to the pleasure of the governments which they represent. The Reichstag, however, like the Canadian House of Commons, which is elected for a period of five years, may be dissolved before the expiration of the term set by law for its duration.

In democratic Switzerland, the constitution places certain restrictions on the election of officers of the legislative assemblies, with the view of distributing the honor and power attaching to the positions. The National Council, or lower house, elects from its members " for each regular or extra session a president and a vice-president. The member who has been president during one regular session cannot, at the following regular session, occupy this position or that of the vice-president. Nor can the same person be vice-president during two consecutive regular sessions."[1] In the Swiss Senate, the president and vice-president are elected under the same conditions as the officers of the lower house, but " neither the president nor the vice-president can be elected from the senators of the canton from which the president was chosen for the regular session immediately preceding. Nor can vice-presidents for two consecutive regular sessions be chosen from the senators of the same canton."[2] In the elections of both houses the president votes as the other members, and, moreover, decides in case of a tie. But in the less democratic United States, the House of Representatives

[1] Federal Constitution of Switzerland, Art. 78.
[2] *Ibid.*, Art. 82.

112   GOVERNMENT OF SWITZERLAND.

elects its speaker without any of those restrictions which are imposed in Switzerland ; so that whatever power may be exercised through the speaker may be wielded by one State for a long series of years. But the Senate has no voice in the choice of its speaker, inasmuch as the vice-president of the United States is the president of the Senate. He has no vote, however, except in case of a tie.

In the organization of its legislative assemblies Canada follows more or less closely the practice of the English Parliament. " The speaker of the Senate is appointed by a commission under the great seal."[1] In the words of the British North America Act, "the governor-general may from time to time, by instrument under the great seal of Canada, appoint a senator to be speaker of the Senate, and may remove him and appoint another in his stead."[2] The speaker of the Canadian House of Commons is elected by the house with ceremonies similar to those which accompany the election of a speaker of the Commons of England.[3]

With respect to the payment of the members of federal legislatures, a varied practice prevails. In the German Empire there is a constitutional

[1] Bourinot, " Parliamentary Procedure and Practice," 157.
[2] Article 34.
[3] Bourinot, " Parliamentary Procedure and Practice," 224–230.

provision which affirms that "the members of the Reichstag shall not be allowed to draw any salary or be compensated as such."[1] The members of the Bundesrath, however, in this regard are subject to such conditions as the individual States may see fit to impose. But in Switzerland, the members of the lower house are paid out of the federal treasury, while those of the Senate, or Council of States, are paid by the cantons. In the majority of cases, as in the United States, Canada, and the South American federations, both houses are paid from the funds of the general government. The usage in Canada is a wide departure from the practice of England, where the members of neither house receive pay. In the Dominion, "the members of both houses receive a sessional indemnity, besides a traveling allowance, and forfeit a certain sum for every day of absence from their duties in the house."[2]

As already indicated, the federal government of Switzerland deals only with such subjects as are placed under its control by the constitution, and of these all are considered by the two houses of the legislature, except those which have been relegated to some other federal authority. A list of the subjects which fall within the competence

[1] Article 32.
[2] Bourinot, "Parliamentary Procedure and Practice," 146.

of the federal legislature is given in the eighty-fifth article of the constitution. It embraces the following:—

1. Laws on the organization and mode of electing the federal authorities;

2. Laws and resolutions on matters which the constitution places in federal hands;

3. The salary and indemnity of the members of the federal government; the creation of permanent offices, and the determination of the salaries attaching to them;

4. The election of the Federal Council, the Federal Tribunal, and the Chancellor, also the commander-in-chief of the federal army. Federal legislation may confer upon the Federal Assembly the right to make and confirm other elections;

5. Alliances and treaties with foreign states as well as the approval of the treaties of the cantons among themselves or with foreign states; yet the treaties of the cantons are not brought before the Federal Assembly unless complaints are raised by the Federal Council or another canton;

6. Measures to provide against danger from without, as also to maintain the independence and neutrality of Switzerland; making war and peace;

7. The guarantee of the constitutions and the

territory of the cantons; intervention in consequence of this guarantee; measures for the internal security of Switzerland, for the maintenance of tranquillity and order; amnesty and the right of pardon;

8. Measures to insure respect for the federal constitution, to make effective the guarantee of the cantonal constitutions, as well as those measures which have for their end the fulfillment of federal duties;

9. The control of the federal army;

10. The determination of the annual budget. The approval of the public expenditures, and resolutions authorizing loans;

11. The supreme control of the administration and the federal courts;

12. Charges against the decisions of the federal council concerning administrative contests (Art. 113);

13. Questions of jurisdiction between federal authorities;

14. The revision of the federal constitution.

This list is not to be taken as a strictly exhaustive indication of the powers of the Federal Assembly. In this respect it may be likened to the eighth section of the first article of the Constitution of the United States. It appears, however, from this enumeration that the Federal Assembly exercises not only legislative power, but also supervisory (11), executive (8, 9, 10), and judicial (12, 13) power; but the judicial functions of the Federal Assembly at present are less extensive than those enjoyed by this body under the constitution of 1848.

According to the constitution, the two houses of the legislature are required to assemble in ordinary session once each year, on a day fixed by law. Still it has become customary for them to assemble regularly for longer meetings in June and December, and besides to hold shorter sessions whenever the business may require it.[1] The extra sessions are held at the call of the Federal Council, or on the demand of a fourth of the members of the lower house, or on that of five cantons.[2] Ordinarily each house sits separately, but for the purpose of electing the officers mentioned in Art. 85, Sec. 4, and for exercising the right of pardon, or deciding in cases of disputed jurisdiction, the two houses assemble in joint session, the president of the lower house presiding, and decisions are determined by the majority of the members of the two houses voting. The initiative belongs to each house, to each individual member, and also to the cantons. The meetings are generally public. The members of both houses vote without instructions, and enjoy the usual privi-

[1] Von Orelli, 32.
[2] Article 86.

leges and immunities of members of representative bodies. The quorum in each house consists of a majority of all the members, and measures are adopted by an absolute majority of those voting. In passing laws, decrees, and resolutions, each house has a veto on the action of the other; in other words, in order to reach a positive decision the two bodies must be in accord. But such agreement is not adequate in all cases to the establishment of a law. Whenever it is demanded by 30,000 active citizens, or by eight cantons, the federal law passed by the two houses must be submitted to the people to be adopted or rejected by them. This is also the case with federal resolutions which have a general bearing, and which are not regarded as urgent.[1] It is left to federal legislation to determine what is necessary with respect to the form and the times for the popular voting.[2]

In June, 1874, a few days after the adoption of the amended constitution, a federal law was passed, making provision for carrying out the principle of referendum, which had been established by Art. 89.

According to this provision, laws and resolutions, on which a popular vote might be demanded, were to be published immediately after their passage, and copies were to be sent to the

[1] Article 89.
[2] Article 90.

governments of the several cantons. Through the cantons they were then to be brought to the attention of the communes. It was, moreover, required that the demands for a popular vote should be presented to the Federal Council in writing within ninety days after the passage of the law or resolution in question. Every effective demand had to be signed by the citizen making it, signing by proxy being by law forbidden. If at the expiration of the ninety days indicated, the demand was found to have been made in the proper manner by 30,000 voters, the Federal Council fixed a day for taking the popular vote. The voting day was required to be at least four weeks later than the day on which the Federal Council took action determining it. The arrangements for taking the vote were then made by the cantons. The reports of the results of the voting, as made for each commune, embraced the number of those entitled to vote, the number of those who had voted, the number accepting, and the number rejecting, the measure. These original certificates were sent to the Federal Council. If there were neither 30,000 voters nor eight cantons demanding the referendum, or if, in case the popular vote was taken and the proposition of the legislature was accepted, the law was then published in the official list and its execution ordered.

During the first twelve years after the passage of this law, between 1874 and 1886, the federal legislature passed 113 laws and resolutions which were capable of being submitted to the referendum. Of these only 19 were subjected to the popular vote, and of these last 13 were rejected and 6 adopted.

The strong opposing views, which are held in Switzerland regarding the expediency of the referendum, indicate that this is one of the features of the government which is open to future discussion. On the one hand, it may be claimed that the representative system is of supreme importance, and that the referendum is inconsistent with it, and, if carried out, will lead to its subversion. On the other hand, it is asserted that "the combination of representative institutions, with the direct exercise of popular sovereignty, is well calculated to promote the welfare of a people occupying the peculiar position in which the Swiss are placed. The discipline of self-government in the commune, and the training afforded by an effective system of education, have qualified them for the practice of direct democracy in the cantons and in the Confederation. The chief drawback of the referendum consists in the possible diminution of the feeling of responsibility in the members of the representative assemblies. That disadvantage, however, is amply outweighed by the educative effect which the system exercises on the great bulk of the citizens, by disposing them to recognize the necessity for the careful discharge of the duties involved in their rights, and by inspiring them with constant solicitude for the well-being of the state to which they belong."[1]

[1] *Westminster Review*, Feb., 1888, p. 213.

CHAPTER V.

THE EXECUTIVE.

THE development of a federal government from a loose confederacy is attended by the growth of the executive as a separate department of the state. In the United States before 1787, and in Switzerland before 1848, the legislative and the executive powers were vested in the same body. Under the organization of existing federal states the executive exists as a separate department of government, and in the federal republics as a department separate but co-ordinate with the judicial and legislative departments. Although the existing federal governments are brought together into a single class, they are, nevertheless, marked by wide variations with respect to the details of organization. These variations are as conspicuous, perhaps, with reference to the executive department as any other. In Canada and the German Empire, the head of the executive department is constituted by the right of inheritance; while in the United States, Mexico,

Colombia, Venezuela, the Argentine Republic, and Switzerland, he holds his position by virtue of either a direct or an indirect election.

"The executive government and authority of and over Canada" is vested in the queen, and is consequently subjected to the law of succession prevailing in England. The direct agent of the queen in exercising this government and authority in the dominion is a governor-general, appointed by letters-patent under the great seal. "His jurisdiction and powers are defined by the terms of his commission, and by the royal instructions which accompany the same. He holds office during the pleasure of the Crown, but he may exercise his functions for at least six years from the time he has entered on his duties. In all his communications with the imperial government, of which he is an officer, he addresses the secretary of state for the colonies, the constitutional avenue through which he must approach the sovereign."[1] On entering upon his duties, he takes "the necessary oaths of allegiance and office before the chief justice, or any other judge of the supreme court of the dominion," and causes his commission to be formally read.[2] He "is authorized, among other things, to exercise all powers lawfully belonging to the queen, with respect to the summoning, proroguing,

[1] Bourinot, "Parliamentary Procedure and Practice," 49.
[2] *Ibid.*, 50.

or dissolving parliament; to administer the oaths of allegiance and office; to transmit to the imperial government copies of all laws assented to by him or reserved for the signification of the royal assent; to administer the prerogative of pardon; to appoint all ministers of state, judges, and other public officers, and to remove or suspend them for sufficient cause. He may also appoint a deputy or deputies to exercise certain of his powers and functions. He may not leave the dominion upon any pretense whatsoever without having first obtained permission to do so through one of the principal secretaries of state. In case of the death, incapacity, removal or absence from Canada of the governor-general, his powers are vested in a lieutenant-governor or administrator appointed by the queen, under the royal sign-manual; or, if no such appointment has been made, in the senior officer in command of the imperial troops in the dominion."[1]

The president of the German federation is the King of Prussia, who bears the title of German Emperor. "He shall represent the empire among nations, declare war, and conclude peace in the name of the same, enter into alliances and other conventions with foreign countries, accredit ambassadors and receive them. For a declara-

[1] Bourinot, 51; British North America Act, Articles 9-16.

tion of war in the name of the empire the consent of the Bundesrath shall be required, except in case of an attack upon the territory of the confederation or its coasts." Treaties with foreign powers, made by the emperor and relating to matters under the supervision of the imperial legislature, require the ratification of the Bundesrath and the approval of the Reichstag to render them valid.[1] Such authority as is here vested in the emperor for determining foreign relations, belongs, in the government of Canada, to the British Crown. But, like the governor-general, the emperor has the power of summoning, proroguing, or dissolving the diet.[2] To him belongs "the right to prepare and publish the laws of the empire and the surveillance of their execution."[3] He shall also "appoint the officers of the empire, require them to take the oath of allegiance, and dismiss them when necessary."[4] Moreover, if any State of the empire shall not fulfill its constitutional duties to the empire, proceedings may be instituted against it by execution, "and this execution shall be ordered by the Bundesrath, and enforced by the emperor."[5]

[1] Constitution of the German Empire, Art. 11.
[2] *Ibid.*, Art. 12.
[3] *Ibid.*, Art. 17.
[4] *Ibid.*, Art. 18.
[5] *Ibid.*, Art. 19.

THE EXECUTIVE. 125

Although the president in each of the American federal republics is elected, yet no two of these states have the same method of election. The method established by the Constitution of the United States is set forth in the second clause of Article 2, and in the Twelfth Amendment: "Each State shall appoint, in such manner as the legislature thereof may direct, a number of electors equal to the whole number of senators and representatives to which the State may be entitled in the Congress." The manner of appointment was not determined by the constitution, but left to the legislature of each State. At first they were "chosen in four different modes, namely, by joint ballot of the State legislatures, by a concurrent vote of the two branches of the State legislature, by the people of the State voting by general ticket, and by the people voting in districts."[1] The existing practice is a combination of the last two modes. "The electors shall meet in their respective States, and vote by ballot for president and vice-president, one of whom, at least, shall not be an inhabitant of the same State with themselves; they shall name in their ballots the person voted for as president, and in distinct ballots the person voted for as vice-president." The ballots shall be counted by the president of

[1] Lanman's "Directory of Congress," 427.

the Senate in the presence of the Senate and House of Representatives. "The person having the greatest number of votes for president shall be the president, if such number be a majority of the whole number of electors appointed; and if no person have such majority, then from the persons having the highest numbers, not exceeding three, on the list of those voted for as president, the House of Representatives shall choose immediately by ballot, the president. But in choosing the president the votes shall be taken by States, the representation from each State having one vote; a quorum for this purpose shall consist of a member or members from two-thirds of the States, and a majority of all the States shall be necessary to a choice. And if the House of Representatives shall not choose a president whenever the right of choice shall devolve upon them, before the fourth day of March next following, then the vice-president shall act as president, as in case of the death or other constitutional disability of the president. The person having the greatest number of votes as vice-president shall be the vice-president, if such number be a majority of the whole number of electors appointed; and if no person have a majority, then, from the two highest numbers on the list, the Senate shall choose the vice-president; a quorum for the purpose shall consist of two-thirds of the whole number of senators, and a majority of the whole number shall be necessary to a choice."

"The Congress may determine the time of choosing the electors, and the day on which they shall give their votes, which day shall be the same throughout the United States."

By the framers of this law it was intended that the electors should freely choose and appoint the presidents, but the practice has departed so widely from the original intention that the electors are now only a definite number of votes determined for one or the other candidate by the suffrages of the people. The result of the existing method is unlike that of a direct vote, inasmuch as by preserving the individuality of certain districts and groups of districts, it becomes possible for a minority of the actual voters to elect the president.[1]

In Mexico, to use the language of the constitution, "the election of president shall be indirect in the first degree and by secret ballot, under conditions fixed by the electoral law."[2] The electoral law providing for the election of president is that already detailed, as providing for the election of deputies, senators, and members

[1] See Pomeroy, "Introduction to Municipal Law," § 731; also, Pomeroy, "Constitutional Law," 130–133; Dicey, "The Law of the Constitution," 29–30.

[2] Article 76.

of the Supreme Court, as well as for the president of the Republic.[1]

The constitution of the republic of Colombia provides that "the election of the president of the Union shall be made by the vote of the States, each State having one vote, which shall be that of the relative majority of its respective electors, in accordance with its laws. The congress shall declare elected president the citizen who obtains the absolute majority of the votes of the States. In case no one has such a majority, the congress shall elect from those who have received the larger numbers of votes."[2] The congress, into whose hands the election falls under certain conditions, is defined by the constitution to be "the House of Representatives and the Senate taken collectively."[3] In comparing this method of election with that followed in the United States, it will be observed that each State has only one vote instead of having a number equal to its congressional representation, and that, in case of failure on the part of the college to elect, the power to choose a president falls to the two houses in joint session rather than to the lower house, as in the United States. The framers of the Constitution of Colombia, like the makers of the United States

[1] See pp. 102-103, *ante*.
[2] Article 75.
[3] Article 48.

Constitution, desired to emphasize the individuality of the States, and in giving to each a single vote, they made the probability of a president's election by a minority of the voters much greater than in the United States. If this evil were avoided by making the vote of the people for the president immediate, the power of determining the election might remain permanently in the hands of a few of the larger States.

The method of electing a president, which is observed in Colombia, is followed in every essential particular in the Republic of Venezuela. The citizens of each State vote by a direct and secret ballot, the relative majority in each State determining the vote of the State, which counts as one in the election. An absolute majority of all the States is required; and when no candidate has this number, the election is made by the congress from those who have received the highest numbers of votes. But in the Argentine Republic, the provisions of the constitution relating to the election of a president are not greatly unlike those set forth in the Constitution of the United States. A conspicuous point of difference, however, is found in the fact that the electoral college is relatively larger in the former state than in the latter. According to Article 81, " the capital and each of the provinces shall appoint by a direct vote a college of electors, equal to twice the number of deputies and senators which they send to congress, with the same qualifications and under the same forms, which are prescribed for the election of deputies.

"The electors having met in the capital of the nation, and in that of their respective provinces, four months before the close of the presidential term, shall proceed to elect the president and vice-president of the nation by signed tickets, indicating in one the person for whom they vote for president, and in another the person whom they choose for vice-president." The course pursued in determining the result of such an election is the same as that provided in the twelfth amendment of the United States Constitution, but, in case of failure on the part of the electors to elect a president the choice shall fall to the congress rather than, as in the United States, to the House of Representatives.

The qualifications required by the Constitution of the United States for the office of president, are that the candidate shall be "a natural-born citizen," thirty-five years of age, and have "been fourteen years a resident within the United States."[1] Essentially the same qualifications are required in Mexico, where he must be "a Mexican citizen by birth, in the exercise

[1] Article 2.

THE EXECUTIVE. 131

of his rights, thirty-five years of age, not an ecclesiastic, and reside in the country at the time of his election."[1] The Constitution of Colombia makes no mention of qualifications, and that of Venezuela simply states that he must be a citizen of Venezuela by birth, and thirty years of age.[2] This lower minimum of age is also one of the qualifications in the Argentine Republic, where, besides, it is required that the candidate shall have been born within the limits of the Argentine territory, or be the son of a citizen by birth, belong to the Roman Catholic communion, and be in receipt of an annual income of two thousand dollars.[3]

The term of the presidential office in the several federations varies from one to six years. It is one year in Colombia, two years in Venezuela, four years in the United States and Mexico, and six years in the Argentine Republic. In case of the removal of the president from office, or of his death, resignation, or inability to discharge the powers and duties of the office, these powers and duties shall devolve on the vice-president in the United States and the Argentine Republic. In case of the removal, death, resignation, or inability of both the pres-

[1] Constitution of Mexico, Art. 77.
[2] Constitution of Venezuela, Art. 62.
[3] Argentine Constitution, Art. 76 and 47.

ident and the vice-president, the congress shall determine what officer shall then act as president, until the disability be removed, or a president shall be elected.[1] In the other members of this group of states, the office of vice-president is wanting. In case of the vacancy of the presidential office in Mexico, the president of the supreme court exercises the powers belonging to the president. In like case in Colombia, the title and powers of president are assumed by one of three persons whom the congress, by absolute majority, elects each year for this purpose.[2] A merely temporary vacancy in Venezuela is supplied by one of the ministers elected by his colleagues; but when the vacancy is caused by death, resignation, removal, or termination of the period of election, the president of the supreme court shall take in charge the executive office, and call an election, "at least when the vacancy occurs within the last six months of the constitutional period."[3]

Under a democratic *régime* there is manifest a reluctance to continue any person in the same office for a number of terms. The laws and practices of the federal states under considera-

[1] Article 75 of the Argentine Constitution, and the sixth section of Article 2 of the United States Constitution, which treat of this topic, contain essentially the same statement.
[2] Article 65.
[3] Article 67.

tion illustrate this statement. In Colombia and the Argentine Republic a person cannot be re-elected president for the constitutional term immediately following that during which he has occupied that office. In Venezuela this prohibition extends not only to the person who has been president, but also to his relatives to the fourth degree of consanguinity. The same provision as in the Argentine Republic and Colombia existed also in the Mexican constitution, until by a recent amendment of Article 78 the president became eligible to a re-election for the constitutional period immediately following; but at the close of his second term he becomes disqualified for the office until four years have elapsed, counting from the date of his ceasing to exercise the functions of the office. On the point in question, the Constitution of the United States is silent, but a " constitutional understanding,"[1] as Professor Dicey calls it, has come into existence to the effect that no president shall be re-elected more than once.

In contrast with the organization of this department in other federal states, the executive authority in Switzerland is exercised by a federal council composed of seven members.[2] The members of this council are elected for a period

[1] "The Law of the Constitution," 29.
[2] Swiss Federal Constitution, Art. 95.

of three years by the two legislative assemblies in joint session, and any Swiss citizen eligible to the lower house may be elected. But only one member may be selected from a single canton. The Federal Council is renewed entirely after each renewal of the lower house of the legislature. Vacancies occurring during the term of election are filled by the Federal Assembly, at its next session, for the unexpired portion of the term.[1] While in office the members of the council are not permitted to follow any business or profession, or to have any other employment either in the service of the Federation or in a canton.[2] The Federal Assembly, the body which elects the members of the council, appoints one of them to be its presiding officer, who is called "the president of the confederation." Another member is appointed by the same body to be "the vice-president of the federal council." Both "the president of the confederation" and "the vice-president of the federal council" are appointed for one year. The same member may not be vice-president two years in succession; and the president having served one term is not permitted to be either president or vice-president for the year immediately following.[3] The president and the

[1] Swiss Federal Constitution, Art. 96.
[2] *Ibid.*, Art. 97.
[3] *Ibid.*, Art. 98.

other members of the Federal Council receive an annual salary from the federal treasury.[1] The presence of four members of the council is required for the transaction of business.[2] The members of the Federal Council have a consultative voice in the legislative assemblies, and also the right to make propositions on subjects there under consideration.[3]

On the Federal Council devolve most of the important powers that usually belong to the executive in a federal state. It directs the affairs of the Federation in accordance with federal laws and resolutions. It sees to it that these laws and resolutions and the federal constitution are observed; makes effective the guarantee of the cantonal constitutions; presents to the federal legislature projects of laws and resolutions; gives its opinion on propositions which are addressed to it by the legislative assemblies or by the cantons; provides for the execution of the federal laws and resolutions, the judgments of the federal tribunal, and the agreements reached by arbitration between the cantons. It makes the appointments which are not attributed to the Federal Assembly, to the Federal Tribunal, or to any other authority. It examines

[1] Swiss Federal Constitution, Art. 99.
[2] *Ibid.*, Art. 100.
[3] *Ibid.*, Art. 101.

and approves the treaties of the cantons between themselves or with a foreign power. It watches over the interests of the Federation in international affairs; guards the security of Switzerland against external dangers, and maintains its independence and neutrality. It, moreover, watches over the internal security of the Federation, and the maintenance of tranquillity and order. In case of urgency, and when the legislature is not in sesson, the Federal Council is authorized to raise the necessary troops, and to direct them, under the obligation to convoke the legislative assemblies immediately, and provided the number of troops raised does not exceed two thousand men, and they do not remain more than three weeks under arms. It is charged with the concerns of the federal army, and with all other branches of the administration, which pertain to the Federation. It examines the laws and ordinances of the cantons, which must be submitted for its approval; and exercises surveillance over those branches of cantonal administration which are placed under its control. It administers the finances of the Federation, proposes the budget, and renders an account of receipts and expenses. It superintends the action of all the functionaries and employees of the federal administration. It renders an account of its action to the Federal Assembly, at each regular session, presents to it a report on the condition of internal and external affairs, and recommends legislative action on such measures as appear to be useful for increasing the common prosperity. It makes also special reports whenever the Federal Assembly or one of its sections demands it.[1]

The affairs which thus fall to the Federal Council are distributed by the council itself among the several members. One has the affairs of the interior, one justice and police, one war, one the treasury, one commerce and agriculture, and one the post-office and a general supervision over the railways. The president of the council is nominally president of the Federation, yet his legal powers are only those of a member of a council where in "theory each is responsible for all, and all are responsible for each." "In the hands, however, of a man of great ability, the position assumes far more importance than would appear likely from a mere analysis of the functions which the constitution calls upon him to perform; for it must be borne in mind that, not only is he intrusted with a certain control over the various departments of the executive, and not only does he represent Switzerland in the eyes of foreign nations, and has frequently in that capacity to

[1] Swiss Federal Constitution, Art. 102.

take the initiative in matters of general policy, but his personal influence is felt within the Federal Assembly itself."[1] The division of the Federal Council into departments is, however, only for the sake of facilitating the examination and dispatch of business; the decisions emanate from the council as a unit. It has all the solidarity of the English Cabinet and a more secure tenure of office. Its members may take part in the debates of the two houses of the legislature, but are not obliged to retire on losing legislative confidence. Although practically a committee of the legislature for executive purposes, it is still endowed with a good degree of independence. Mr. Freeman calls attention to the fact that the Swiss houses " do formally, at the beginning of each Parliament, what the English House of Commons does silently; that is, they determine whether the existing ministry shall remain in office. There is indeed the difference that a Federal Council or Councillor, when once chosen, cannot be got rid of for three years, except in case of actual crime. Still the relations between the Federal Council and the two houses come nearer to the English model than they do to the totally independent position of the American President and Congress."[2]

[1] *Westminster Review*, Feb., 1888, p. 208.
[2] *Fortnightly Review*, II, 542.

Finally, the Federal Council and its departments are authorized to call experts for special objects.[1]

[1] Swiss Federal Constitution, Art. 104.

CHAPTER VI.

THE JUDICIARY.

BEFORE a union of States is entitled to the position of a *Bundesstaat*, or federal state, it must be clothed with authority to exert sovereign power directly upon the individual citizens of the several States; and a necessary means for thus exercising this power is a court or a system of courts existing as a part of the federal organism. In the United States, the Constitution established merely one supreme court, but provided for the existence of "such inferior courts as the Congress may from time to time ordain and establish."[1] The organization of the Supreme Court, including the power to fix the number of the judges, was left to Congress, but the appointment of the judges was placed in the hands of the President, acting with the advice and consent of the Senate. It was, moreover, provided that "the judges, both of the

[1] U. S. Constitution, Art. 3, Sec. 1.

supreme and inferior courts, shall hold their offices during good behavior."[1] As at present organized, the Supreme Court consists of one chief justice and eight associate justices, any six of whom shall constitute a quorum.[2]

Of the supreme courts of the Spanish-American federations, that of the Argentine Republic, with respect to its organization, most nearly resembles that of the United States. Here "the judicial power of the nation," to use the language of the Argentine constitution, "shall be exercised by a supreme court of justice, and by other inferior tribunals which the congress may establish within the territory of the nation." As in the United States, moreover, "the judges of the supreme court and of the inferior courts shall be appointed by the president, with the consent of the senate, shall hold their offices during good behavior, and shall receive for their services a. compensation which the law shall determine, and which shall not be diminished in any manner while they continue in office."[3] In the Argentine Republic, however, there are limitations on the appointment

[1] U. S. Constitution, Art. 3, Sec. 1.

[2] Revised Statutes of the United States (1878), Sec. 673.

[3] Constitution of the Argentine Republic, Arts. 86, 94, and 96; see also United States Constitution, Art. 3; Constitution of Colombia, Art. 86.

of judges which do not exist in the United States. In the latter country any citizen may be made a justice of the Supreme Court, but in the former country no one shall become a member of the Supreme Court of Justice who is not an advocate of at least eight years of practice, and has, moreover, the qualifications required for a senator.[1]

The professional conditions required in the Argentine Republic are wanting in both Colombia and Venezuela. In Colombia, no conditions are prescribed, except that of the five justices of the supreme court not more than one shall be taken from a single State at the same time.[2] The article of the constitution which creates the supreme court of Colombia, provides that the judicial power shall be exercised also by the senate and by the tribunals of the States, and by those which are established in the territories. In Venezuela, however, the qualifications required for the position of justice of the supreme federal court are: (1) That the candidate shall be a citizen of Venezuela by birth or have been ten years naturalized; (2) that he shall be thirty years of age. The supreme court in each of these states is composed of five justices, and the number is fixed by the constitution, instead of

[1] Argentine Constitution, Art. 97.
[2] Constitution of Colombia, Art. 70.

being left to the determination of the national legislature, as in the United States and the Argentine Republic. The method of appointment in these cases is also unlike that of the other States. It is essentially the same in both. The legislature of each State presents to the congress a list of persons in number equal to the number of the places to be filled, and the congress declares elected those who have received the highest number of votes.[1] In Venezuela the votes are counted in five groups of States,[2] while in Colombia all the votes presented are counted together. In case of a tie vote in Colombia, the decision is made by lot, while in Venezuela it is made by the congress. If for any cause whatever the States shall not have presented the lists as required, the congress shall elect to supply the lack until the propositions are sent to it.[3]

The framers of the Mexican constitution, in

[1] Constitution of Colombia, Art. 76; Constitution of Venezuela, Art. 86.

[2] Constitution of Venezuela, Art. 86; these groups are:—
1. Cumaná, Nueva Esparta, Maturin, and Barcelona.
2. Guayana, Apure, Zamora, and Portuguesa.
3. Bolívar, Gusman Blanco, Guárico, and Carabobo.
4. Cojédes, Yaracui, Barquisimento, and Falcon.
5. Zulia, Trujillo, Guzman, and Táchira.

[3] Constitution of Colombia, Art. 76; Constitution of Venezuela, Art. 86.

treating of the federal judiciary, appear to have taken as their model the federal courts of the United States in the form into which they have been brought by the provision of the Constitution and subsequent congressional legislation; for, in Article 90, it is provided that "the exercise of the judicial power of the Federation shall be deposited in one supreme court of justice and in district and circuit courts." The Mexican congress has little power over the federal courts in comparison with that exercised by the congress in the United States. The creation of the district and circuit courts is not left to the will of congress, but is determined by the constitution. The number of judges of the supreme court is fixed at eleven by the constitution, and not left to the determination of the federal legislature. These judges are elected for a term of six years, by an indirect election, in a manner prescribed by a general electoral law, as already indicated.[1] Besides the eleven "judges proprietary," the organization of the supreme court embraces four supernumerary judges, one attorney-general, and one solicitor-general. To be eligible to membership in the supreme court, the candidate "must be instructed in the science of the law, according to the judgment of the

---

[1] See pp. 102 and 103, *ante*.

THE JUDICIARY. 145

electors, more than thirty-five years of age, and a Mexican citizen by birth, in the enjoyment of his rights."[1] "The duties of a member of the supreme court cannot be resigned except for grave reason, approved by the congress, to whom the resignation must be presented."[2] In case the congress is not in session, approval must be rendered by the permanent deputation.

Under the British North America Act, the Parliament of Canada was authorized to "provide for the constitution, maintenance, and organization of a general court of appeal for Canada, and for the establishment of any additional courts for the better administration of the laws of Canada."[3] To carry out this provision, a bill to create a supreme court for the dominion was introduced into the Canadian parliament in 1875. "It was the expressed intention of ministers to have prohibited any further appeals to her Majesty's privy council. They were notified, however, that the bill could not be sanctioned unless it preserved to the Crown its rights to hear the appeals of all British subjects, who might desire to appeal in the ultimate resort to the queen in council. Accordingly, a saving clause to that effect was in-

[1] Constitution of Mexico, Art. 93.
[2] *Ibid.*, Art. 95.
[3] British North America Act, Art. 101.

serted in the bill, and it received the royal assent."[1] The court thus created comprises a chief justice and five associate judges, who are appointed by the governor-general, and who hold office during good behavior. The Canadian procedure in legislating suggests that of Great Britain, but the decisions of the Canadian parliament are subject to a judicial control which is wholly unknown in England, and which suggests the practice of the United States. "In Great Britain the legislature is the chief power in the land. There being no written constitution, no plain-speaking and inflexible statute of paramount law, under which the government of the country is carried on, the constitutionality of its acts cannot be questioned by the courts in the same way as in those countries wherein there is a written constitution. The acts of the legislature form the law, which the courts must execute without questioning their validity or testing them with the constitution. The British people speak in each legislative enactment; and their last utterance is the guide for their courts, who are always subordinate to the legislature, and who exist solely by their permission. These imperial enactments extend at times to the Colonies; and there Her Majesty's courts are precisely in

[1] Todd, "Parliamentary Government in the British Colonies," 150.

THE JUDICIARY. 147

the same position, so far as these enactments are concerned. They have the same duties under them as the British courts have to see that they are carried out according to law."

"An imperial statute in 1867 gave Canada a written and defined constitution.[1] Under this constitution numerous bodies were endowed with large legislative powers. All the laws were to be executed by the courts, but executed so as not to conflict with the imperial laws, which must, first of all, be executed. Our courts, therefore, while bound to execute all laws in force, must be the judges as to what laws are in force. A Canadian law which is repugnant to any imperial enactment must be declared void by the courts—a higher than Canadian power has said that it is no law at all. Again, the dominion parliament may usurp provincial rights, or a province assume to deal with dominion matters; the courts still sitting under the constitution, the imperial enactment, must refuse to obey their behests. The courts in Canada are still the queen's courts and bound to execute such law as is in force, but equally bound to declare that the act of any of our legislatures, when transcending their limits, is unconstitutional and void. The courts, so long as

[1] The British North America Act, 1867; see Bourinot, 699–739.

they are permitted to exist, are not the creatures of the legislature; they are of course subordinate to constitutional legislation, but they are co-ordinate and in effect superior to that which is not constitutional."[1]

The relation which the Canadian courts hold to imperial legislation is, in many respects, the same as that which the courts of the United States hold to the federal constitution. The position of the Canadian courts may, moreover, be regarded as a result of imitation rather than of inheritance and tradition. In creating the supreme court, it was intended that it "should serve as a court of appeal from the provincial courts, and likewise possess original jurisdiction as an exchequer court in revenue causes, and other cases in which the Crown is interested." It has also acquired jurisdiction "for the trial of suits against the Crown in Canada by petition of right." The governor in council may, moreover, "refer any matters whatsoever to the court for hearing or consideration; and the judges are required to examine and report upon any private bill, or petition for the same, that may be referred to them by the Senate or House of Commons of the dominion. It is also provided that, when the legislature of any province in Canada shall have passed an act agreeing to the

[1] O'Sullivan, "Government in Canada," 194-196.

THE JUDICIARY. 149

exercise by the supreme court of jurisdiction in controversies between the dominion and any such province, or between any two or more provinces; or, in suits wherein the question of the validity of a dominion or provincial statute is material to the decision thereof, then the supreme court shall exercise jurisdiction in regard to such matters."[1]

The supreme court is the highest court of appeal in Canada, "and entertains appeals within and throughout the dominion from the last court of resort in the provinces. By leave, however, it may hear an appeal from any decree, decretal, or order made by a court of equity, or in an equity proceeding or any final judgment of the superior courts, other than those of Quebec, without intermediate appeal to such last provincial court, providing the case originally commenced in such superior court. In certain cases in election petitions an appeal in the same way will lie to this court. In equity cases, and in proceedings in the nature of equity, an appeal will lie to this court, even from orders made in the exercise of judicial discretion."[2]

Besides the supreme court, there is another dominion court called the Exchequer Court of

[1] Todd, "Parliamentary Government in the British Colonies," 380-381.
[2] O'Sullivan, 208.

Canada. It "looks after the revenue of the country, enforces certain penalties on behalf of the Crown, and has jurisdiction in all cases in which demand shall be made or relief sought in respect of any matter which might in England be the subject of a suit or action in the court of exchequer on its plea side against any officer of the Crown. It also deals exclusively with those cases which, in the English exchequer court, were instituted on its revenue side against the Crown."[1] The supreme court judges are the judges of the exchequer court, and "cases are heard before a single judge in the first instance with or without a jury, and an appeal lies to the supreme court."[2]

In Canada the dominion legislature has not only organized the federal courts but also determined the extent of their jurisdiction. But in the United States only the organization of the courts is left to the Congress; the extent of their power is fixed by the terms of the Constitution, and the Congress cannot increase or diminish it. As provided in the second section of Article 3 of the Constitution of the United States, "the judicial power shall extend to all cases, in law and equity, arising under this Constitution, the laws of the United States, and treaties made, or

[1] O'Sullivan, 214.
[2] O'Sullivan, 215.

THE JUDICIARY. 151

which shall be made, under their authority; to all cases affecting ambassadors, other public ministers, and consuls; to all cases of admiralty and maritime jurisdiction; to controversies to which the United States shall be a party; to controversies between two or more States, between a State and citizens of another State, between citizens of different States, between citizens of the same State claiming lands under grants of different States, and between a State, or the citizens thereof, and foreign states, citizens, or subjects." In some of these cases the Supreme Court has original, and in others only appellate, jurisdiction. The line of distinction between these two classes of cases is drawn by the second paragraph of the section from which the previous quotation is made: " In all cases affecting ambassadors, other public ministers, and consuls, and those in which a State shall be a party, the Supreme Court shall have original jurisdiction." This means that the Supreme Court shall have original jurisdiction in the cases here mentioned and no other.[1] " In all the other cases before mentioned, the Supreme Court shall have appellate jurisdiction, both as to law and fact, with such exceptions and under such regulations as the Congress shall make."

[1] Marbury v. Madison, 1 Cranch, 137; Curtis, " Jurisdiction of the United States Courts," 8.

A case "between a State and citizens of another State" can at present arise only when the suit is brought by the State, for by the eleventh amendment to the Constitution it was provided that "the judicial power of the United States shall not be construed to extend to any suit, in law or equity, commenced or prosecuted against one of the United States by citizens of another State, or by citizens or subjects of any foreign state." A State, however, may be sued by another State or by a foreign sovereign.[1] The appellate jurisdiction of the Supreme Court is exercised over the inferior courts of the United States, and over the courts of the several States.

In determining the jurisdiction of the federal courts of Mexico, the constitution follows in general the provisions of the United States Constitution. The federal tribunals take cognizance of: (1) "All controversies which arise in regard to the fulfillment and application of the federal laws; (2) all cases pertaining to maritime law; (3) those in which the Federation may be a party; (4) those that may arise between two or more States; (5) those that may arise between a State and one or more citizens of another State; (6) civil or criminal cases that may arise under treaties with foreign powers; (7) cases concerning diplomatic agents and

[1] Curtis, 18.

consuls."[1] The Mexican supreme court has original jurisdiction in those cases which arise between States, those in which the Union is a party, and those concerning controversies as to jurisdiction among the federal courts, between the federal and State courts, and between the courts of different States. In all the other cases the supreme court has authority only as a court of appeal.[2] The provisions regarding the jurisdiction of the federal courts which are embodied in the constitutions of Mexico and the United States, are reproduced in all essential particulars in the constitution of the Argentine Republic. In all these cases the constitutional law alone determines the jurisdiction of the federal courts, but in Colombia and Venezuela this is left in part to congressional legislation.

In Switzerland, the articles of agreement between the three Forest districts, formed in 1291, provided that in case of dissension among the parties to the compact, the best and wisest of them should step forward to allay the discord as it should seem to them expedient. If any should reject the action of this self-instituted court, those opposed to the dissatisfied party should unite to support this action. This provision was a recognition of the understanding

[1] Mexican Federal Constitution, Art. 97.
[2] *Ibid.*, Arts. 98–100.

which exists in a small and rude community as to the fitness of certain members to direct the community action to the achievement of certain generally desired ends. It was also a recognition of the fact that power may reside in a community despite the lack of a permanent political organization.

The second phase in the judicial development of the Confederation is seen in the organization of a court of arbitration. This appears with the admission of Zurich into the Union, and was a form of tribunal common to the mediæval city leagues. The number of arbitrators was usually fixed at two for each party, and they met at some neutral point. There being two arbitrators from each side, it was found necessary to provide means to prevent a deadlock, and the most conspicuous means employed was that of appointing an impartial foreman. "The question of the choice of the foreman is unquestionably the main point in the whole system of the courts of arbitration, for generally he was the only real and impartial judge."[1] The difficulties attending the organization of this court prevented its attaining great stability or fulfilling in a satisfactory manner the functions of a general court of the Confederation. The

[1] Dubs," Das Oeffentliche Recht der schweizerischen Eidgenossenschaft," II, 76.

antagonisms of creeds was a prominent obstacle to organized growth in any direction. "After the Reformation several attempts were made by the Diet to give the scheme of arbitration a symmetrical development, but without any practical result. The whole system broke down completely with the old Confederation, but was revived as an organization of the central government with the formation of the articles of confederation, in 1815."[1] The fifth article of this instrument sets forth the system as revived, and in doing so describes more or less accurately an ideal of the institution towards which the Confederation had been striving. In accordance with the provisions of this article, all claims and controversies between the cantons on the subjects not otherwise provided for in the articles of confederation, were turned over to the confederate court. The form and procedure of the suit were as follows: Each of the two cantons in conflict selected from the officers of another canton two arbitrators, or one, if the cantons were agreed in the matter. If the controversy was between more than two cantons, then each party selected the number of arbitrators determined upon. The arbitrators having met, attempted to set aside the conflict in a friendly manner and by way of mediation. If

[1] Dubs, II, 76.

this could not be done, the arbitrators then elected a foreman from the magistrates of some neutral canton not already represented among the arbitrators. If they could not agree in the choice of a foreman, he was appointed by the Diet. In this action of the Diet, however, the cantons in conflict had no voice. The foreman and the arbitrators then attempted once more to allay the strife by arbitration or compromise, but if a settlement could not be reached by these means, they pronounced a decision in accordance with the rights of the parties concerned, at the same time awarding the costs. If necessary, the Diet undertook the execution of the decision thus rendered.[1]

The court of arbitration did not, in any of its forms, satisfy the demand for an impartial and authoritative tribunal. It was, therefore, set aside by the constitution of 1848, and a supreme federal court was organized, consisting of eleven justices and eleven substitutes, one from each canton. These were elected by the Federal Assembly for a term of three years. Provision was made for the annual election of the president and the vice-president of the court, and for the introduction of a jury in criminal cases. It was left to the court itself to deter-

Bundesvertragz wischen den XXII Kantonen der Schweiz, vom 7, August, 1815, Art. 5.

mine its place of meeting. Since the adoption of the amended constitution of 1874, which left to the legislature to determine the organization of the Federal Tribunal, the number of its members, the length of their term of office, and their salaries, the organization of the supreme court has been modified in several particulars. The number of justices and substitutes has been reduced from eleven to nine, and it is provided that the court shall never contain two or more persons from the same family at any given time. The official period has been extended from three to six years, and the president and vice-president are now elected for the terms of two years each. The court elects two court reporters for terms of six years, one of whom must belong to German, and the other to Romance, Switzerland, and of these one is required to be a master of the Italian language; but for the Italian cases, a government secretary belonging to Italian Switzerland is employed. The determination of the place of meeting was left to the Federal Assembly, which, after considering specially the claims of Bern, Lausanne, and Luzern, finally selected Lausanne. The salaries were fixed at ten thousand francs a year for the justices, eleven thousand for the president or chief justice, and from six to eight thousand for the reporters. The president exercises a certain disciplinary function: he may cause persons disturbing the proceedings to be removed from the court-room, and, if need be, imprison them for twenty-four hours. He also exercises supervision over the whole *personnel* of the judiciary department.

As in the United States, there are no professional conditions required, by the constitution, of candidates for the supreme court of Switzerland. "Any Swiss citizen eligible to the lower house of the legislature may be appointed to the Federal Tribunal."[1] Persons ignorant of the law, however, are hardly more likely to be appointed to the supreme court in Switzerland than in the United States. Yet there are restrictions on appointment. These exclude from the list of candidates members of the Federal Council and the Federal Assembly, and all officers holding appointments from these bodies. The members of this tribunal, moreover, are prohibited, during their terms of office, from occupying any other position either in the service of the Federal Government, or in a canton, and they are not permitted to follow any business or profession.

In determining the jurisdiction of the Swiss federal court, Article 113 of the constitution provides that it shall take cognizance of con-

[1] Swiss Federal Constitution, Art. 108.

flicts of competence between the federal and cantonal authorities; of contests between cantons involving constitutional law; of claims for the violation of constitutional rights of the citizens, as well as claims of individuals for violation of concordats or treaties. Administrative controversies are determined by the federal legislature. By this provision a wide field of judicial action is withheld from the sphere of the court. But the action of the court in the cases specified is taken under laws passed by the Federal Assembly, or decrees by this assembly having a general bearing, or treaties ratified by the same authority. Unlike the Supreme Court of the United States, the Swiss federal court has no power to pronounce an act of the federal legislature unconstitutional and void.

Certain points left indefinite by the foregoing constitutional provisions have been determined by subsequent legislation. To note some of these, whenever it is claimed that a case before the federal court falls within the jurisdiction of cantonal authority, or that it should be settled by foreign authority, or by a court of arbitration, the federal court itself decides as to its own competence. On the other hand, questions of jurisdiction between two federal authorities, for example, between the Federal Council and the Federal Tribunal, are decided by the Federal

160 GOVERNMENT OF SWITZERLAND.

Assembly. The Federal Tribunal is called upon to settle boundary questions between two cantons, questions of the application of international treaties, and questions of competence between the authorities of different cantons. It decides in cases of extradition, when the demand is made under an existing treaty, in so far as the application of the treaty is questioned. It takes cognizance, moreover, under conditions established by law, of complaints by private persons and corporations relating, (1) to the violation of those rights which are guaranteed by the federal constitution, by federal legislation enacted to carry out the constitution, or by the constitution of the respective canton; (2) to the violation of agreements among cantons, as well as of treaties with foreign states.[1]

The questions thus far indicated as falling within the jurisdiction of the federal court are constitutional questions. Besides these, the same tribunal takes cognizance of certain civil law cases. These are enumerated in Article 110 of the constitution: "1. Those between the Federation and the cantons. 2. Those between the Federation on the one side and corporations or private persons on the other, when these corporations or these private persons are plaintiffs, and when the case is of the degree of importance

[1] Dubs, II, 88.

required by the federal legislature. 3. Those between cantons. 4. Those between cantons on the one side and corporations or private persons on the other, when the case is of the degree of importance required by federal legislation, and when one of the parties demands it. This court, moreover, decides cases relating to persons without citizenship, also controversies which arise between communes of different cantons touching the right of citizenship." Other cases may be considered by this court when the parties agree to turn them over to it, and when the subject involved is of the degree of importance required by law.[1] In order that a civil case, in which the matter in controversy can be estimated in money, may be brought before the Federal Tribunal on appeal or otherwise, it must involve at least three thousand francs.

The Federal Tribunal acts with the assistance of a jury in certain penal cases which are specified in the 112th article of the constitution as follows: "1. In cases of high treason towards the Federation, of revolt or of violence against the federal authorities; (2) in cases of crimes and misdemeanors under international law; (3) in cases of political crimes and misdemeanors which are the cause or the consequence of disturbances occasioning federal military inter-

[1] Swiss Federal Constitution, Art. 111.

vention; (4) in cases where an officer appointed by federal authority is turned over to the court for a penal judgment."

The judgments of the Federal Tribunal, as well as the decrees of courts of arbitration in intercantonal conflicts, are executed by the Federal Council.[1] To the Federal Assembly, however, belongs the right of amnesty and pardon, with reference to those crimes and misdemeanors which fall within the jurisdiction of the Federal Tribunal.[2]

In commenting on the organization and powers of this court, Professor Dicey points out its weakness as compared with the Supreme Court of the United States. "Nothing," he says, "in the institutions of America has excited more admiration among foreigners than the position given under the Constitution to the federal judiciary. Nothing, on the other hand, is less satisfactory than the position occupied in Switzerland by the Federal Tribunal. That body, it is true, recalls the Supreme Court of the United States, but it has few of the claims to authority possessed by the American court. Its judges are not appointed for life; it is not empowered to adjudicate on the validity of laws passed by the Federal Assembly; it is incom-

[1] Swiss Federal Constitution, Art. 102, Sec. 5.
[2] *Ibid.*, Art. 85, Sec. 7.

petent to deal with many matters which in England, no less than in America, would fall within the jurisdiction of the judges; its decisions are, it would appear, enforced by the action of the executive. The tendency, indeed, of opinion throughout the Confederacy is to strengthen the position of the Federal Tribunal. But even were the authority of the court greatly extended, it would never attain to anything like the power possessed not only by the Supreme Court of America, but even by the English bench. The truth is, that the traditions of Swiss history are unfavorable to the development of that regular supremacy of the law of the land which is the marked characteristic of the institutions founded by the English people an both sides of the Atlantic. The more closely the Swiss federal constitution and the cantonal constitutions of Switzerland are studied, the more apparent it becomes that the tendency of the Swiss people is still, as it has been for centuries, to allow to the legislature the exercise of judicial functions."[1]

[1] *The Nation*, Oct. 8, 1885.

CHAPTER VII.

FOREIGN RELATIONS.

THE twenty-two cantons embraced in the Federation are named in the first article of the constitution, thus making it impossible to increase or diminish the territory of Switzerland except by a constitutional amendment. In the United States the power of annexing territory is exercised by the government under the Constitution. To quote from a decision of the Supreme Court rendered by Chief Justice Marshall, " the Constitution confers absolutely on the government of the Union the power of making war and of making treaties; consequently that government possesses the power of acquiring territory either by conquest or by treaty."[1] If the acquisition is made by conquest, it is presumed that the result will be secured by treaty; and it is to be remembered that the treaty is made, not by Congress, but by the President,

[1] I Pet. 542.

and confirmed by the Senate. The vast power which is here conferred upon the President and the Senate of the United States, in Switzerland is placed directly in the hands of the people. The project of annexation requires there the same direct popular vote which is demanded in case of a proposition to amend the constitution ; and for its acceptance it must have not only a majority of all the votes cast, but also the vote of a majority of the cantons.

The Federation guarantees to the cantons their territories, from which it follows that a canton may not relinquish territory either to a foreign state or to another canton. Such a change can be made only by a change in the federal constitution. In the United States, the transfer of territory from one State to another, or the erection of a new State out of a part or of parts of one or more States, may be effected by Congress and the legislatures of the States concerned. But the government of the United States holds the power to cede to a foreign State a part of the territory of the United States, whether the part so ceded has hitherto been immediately under the dominion of a State or Territorial organization. The Swiss Federation, moreover, guarantees to the cantons their constitutions. In this is involved a guarantee of those powers of the cantons which do not conflict with the powers delegated to the federal government, "the liberty and rights of the people, the constitutional rights of the citizens, and also the rights and prerogatives which the people have conferred upon their officers."[1] The cantons are, in fact, required to seek this federal guarantee, which is accorded under specified conditions: "(1) That the cantonal constitutions contain nothing contrary to the provisions of the federal constitution; (2) that they insure the exercise of political rights under republican forms—representative or democratic; (3) that they have been accepted by the people, and that they may be revised whenever the absolute majority of the citizens demand it."[2]

The carrying out of the first provision is essential to the continued existence of a federal state. A violation of it by a Swiss canton deprives that canton of recognition and protection for its institutions by the Union. In the United States, the power of the Supreme Court to declare void any clause of a State constitution, which is in conflict with the provisions of the federal Constitution, prevents the encroachment of the State on the province of the Federation. The second point, that the Swiss Federation will guarantee only such cantonal

[1] Swiss Federal Constitution, Art. 5.
[2] *Ibid.*, Art. 6.

constitutions as are republican in form, may be compared with the statement of the United States Constitution, that "the United States shall guarantee to every State in this Union a republican form of government."[1] The practical result of introducing this second condition was to require and bring about the organization of Neufchâtel as a republic, which had hitherto existed as a principality under the king of Prussia. The condition that the cantonal constitution must be adopted by the people is a recognition of the democratic foundation of the state, and at the same time it is a constitutional provision to secure practical adherence to this idea. No such provision appears in the fundamental law of the United States, it being presumed instead that the adoption of a State constitution by the people is one of the marks of a republican form of government, which is guaranteed to the State by the federal Constitution. The final clause of the conditions, quoted from Article 6 of the Swiss constitution, namely, that the cantonal constitution must be capable of revision whenever the absolute majority of the citizens demand it, means, "that there must not be constructed any artificial restrictions which would make a revision legally impossible in a case in which a decided popular majority

[1] U. S. Constitution, Art. 4, Sec. 4.

has declared in favor of it. The constitutions which were formed in the period between 1830 and 1848 usually contained the provision that a revision could be made only within designated periods; it might very easily happen that when the period approached there was no need of revision, while, when the people wished a revision, it could not be made without violating the constitution."[1] Such restrictions are, however, no longer permitted.

Under the old confederation the several cantons exercised the right of forming alliances among themselves. But under the Act of Mediation all alliances of one canton with another were prohibited.[2] This prohibition was continued by the articles of alliance of 1815, in so far as such unions were "disadvantageous to the general union or to the rights of other cantons." In the revised draft of 1833, this modifying clause was omitted, and a definite prohibition of all special political alliances between the cantons

---

[1] Blumer, I, 188. Frequently two votes are taken in the canton, one to determine whether or not the constitution shall be revised, the other to accept or reject the revised constitution. The second vote is referred to in the statement of the condition that the cantonal constitutions must be accepted by the people; the first vote, on the other hand, when it is affirmed that they may be revised when the absolute majority of the citizens demand it. Blumer, I. 189;

[2] Article 10.

FOREIGN RELATIONS. 169

introduced. This last provision has been retained in the seventh article of the existing constitution. Yet to the cantons has been left the right to form articles of agreement on subjects of legislation, administration, or justice. It is required, however, that such agreements be subjected to federal control, and to this end they must be brought before the Federal Council.[1] If they are found to contain nothing contrary to the federal laws or to the rights of other cantons they are approved, and in this case the cantons may demand the co-operation of the Federation in their execution. In the contrary case, if such an agreement is not approved, or if another canton raises an objection to it, it must be laid before the Federal Assembly for determination.[2] Questions arising between cantons regarding the interpretation and application of these agreements or compacts between them are brought before the Federal Tribunal for decision.[3]

Whenever independent communities or states unite to form a federal union, thereby giving up some part of their individual authority, an important motive to such a union is the desire for a more efficient agent in the conduct of affairs with foreign states. This motive was conspicu-

[1] Swiss Federal Constitution, Art. 102, Sec. 7.
[2] *Ibid.*, Art. 85, Sec. 5.
[3] *Ibid.*, Art. 113, Sec. 2.

ous in the union of the British colonies in America at each stage of the development of a central power, and not less clearly manifest in the growth of Switzerland from a loose confederacy into a strictly federal state. In America the affairs which called most urgently for a more perfect union were the affairs of trade and finance; but in Switzerland the most prominent aim of the struggle for federalism was the maintenance of security, independence, and neutrality.[1] By the constitution of 1848, the achievement of this end was thrown upon the federal government. To the Federation belongs, moreover, "the right to declare war and make peace; also to make alliances and treaties with foreign states, particularly treaties relating to commerce and customs duties."[2] Not all direct dealings, however, between the individual cantons and foreign powers have been prohibited. "Exceptionally, the cantons preserve the right to make treaties with foreign states on subjects relating to public economy, local relations, and police; nevertheless, these treaties must contain nothing contrary to the Federation or to the rights of other cantons."[3] Questions of conflict under this provision are referred to the Federal Council

---

[1] Swiss Federal Constitution, Art. 85, Sec. 6.
[2] *Ibid.*, Art. 8.
[3] *Ibid.*, Art. 9.

and there settled, unless the council finds objection to them or an objection is raised by another canton, in which case they are brought for settlement before the legislative assemblies. These assemblies, moreover, exercise the rights and powers regarding war, peace, and treaties, which have, by the constitution, been conferred upon the general government.

The question as to the extent of the power which may be exercised by the Union in making treaties under the provisions of Article 8, has been extensively discussed and the conclusion reached that the limitation of powers drawn between the Union and the cantons with respect to internal affairs does not define the powers of the Union with respect to foreign relations. In the treatment of foreign affairs the power of the Union completely overshadows that of the cantons. "The Union in treaties with foreign states is empowered to deal not merely with central matters, but also, in spite of the provisions of Article 3, with subjects whose control belongs otherwise to the cantons; the Union is, however, bound by the other provisions of its constitution particularly those which set forth general political principles, as also those which specifically guarantee to the cantons certain rights."[1]

[1] Blumer, I, 204.

Transactions between Switzerland and foreign states are carried on, on the part of Switzerland, by the Federal Council, whether the affairs under consideration immediately concern individual cantons or the Union.[1] When, however, these transactions relate to public economy, local relations, and public affairs, a canton may deal directly with the inferior authorities and employees of a foreign state.[2]

It devolves upon the Federal Council, moreover, to grant or deny demands made by a foreign power for extradition under an existing treaty; but whenever the application of the treaty is contested, the decision rests with the Federal Tribunal. Under this provision, the Federal Council is subject to certain restrictions. If this body manifests a disposition to comply with the demands of a foreign state, the person whose extradition is sought, or the canton within whose territory he is, may contest the application of the treaty under which the demand is made, and require a decision of the Federal Tribunal in the matter.

The foreign relations of the cantons were to a certain extent influenced by the fact that for a long time Switzerland was a recruiting ground for foreign armies. The stern defenders of re-

[1] Swiss Federal Constitution, Art. 102, Sec. 8 and 9; also Art. 10.
[2] *Ibid.*, Art. 10.

publican liberty at home served all causes abroad. In some important wars they were found on both sides of the conflict. In 1373 three thousand Swiss fought for the duke of Milan against the Pope. They entered the armies of France in large numbers. In 1494 they took part in the expedition of Charles VIII. against Naples, in spite of the orders of the Diet to the contrary. The repeated efforts of the Diet to prevent the Swiss from serving as mercenaries in foreign armies were fruitless. Even solemn agreements among the cantons themselves to abandon the practice were of little avail. In 1503 all of the thirteen cantons united and pledged themselves in a solemn oath to abstain from mercenary engagements with foreign powers; but two years later the Great Council of Bern determined to accept the French subsidy, and sought and received from the Bishop of Lausanne release from the obligations of this oath. In the wars between the French king and the Emperor Maximilian, in 1516, the Swiss fought on both sides. From that time till the present century France continued, with certain brief periods of interruption, to be an important employer of Swiss mercenaries; but at the same time they were found also in the service of many of the other powers. At the time of the wars between France and

Holland in the last decades of the seventeenth century, there were from 25,000 to 30,000 Swiss soidiers in the French army. The whole number in foreign service at this time was not far from 50,000, and it was increased later to about 60,000. The latest instances of this mercenary service were the Swiss regiments in Naples and the Papal States.

Although the mercenary service of the Swiss brought them certain advantages, such as the maintenance of the military spirit and an increase of the material well-being of the participants, it was at the same time attended by serious disadvantages. It tended to destroy the simplicity and sincerity of their national customs and character; it involved them in complicated and dangerous relations with foreign powers; and it made them in a great measure practically dependent on those states whose subsidy they received. Seeing more or less clearly these evil consequences, the central authority as represented in the Diet undertook at various times to abolish the practice, but always with unsatisfactory results. The large measure of independence enjoyed by the several cantons under the old confederation enabled them to disregard with impunity the injunctions of the Diet, and to continue to seek in foreign service their individual profit. The adoption of the federal constitution, however, deprived the several cantons of this power, and placed the general government in a position to correct the abuses which had hitherto existed. By subsequent federal legislation, in 1859, every Swiss citizen was prohibited from entering, without the consent of the Federal Council, those bodies of foreign troops which were not regarded as national troops of the respective states. The purpose of this law was to set aside the disadvantages and dangers which this foreign military service had brought upon Switzerland. These proceeded from the fact that there were certain bodies of troops, who, "bearing the Swiss name, or under Swiss command, or composed for the most part of Swiss soldiers, were fighting for foreign governments, and who were not concerned about the cause which they served, but only about the pay which they received."[1] The law of 1859 had in view specially the abolition of such troops as these, but it did not hinder individual Swiss citizens from enrolling themselves in the national troops of a foreign state. The prohibition was simply to the effect that they could not enter the so-called " Swiss regiments" in foreign service and " Swiss foreign legions," without the permission of the Federal Council.

[1] Blumer, I, 225.

The foreign relations of Switzerland under the confederation were further complicated by the reception of foreign pensions, titles, and orders, by influential Swiss citizens. When these persons obtained positions of power at home, the fact that they were pensioners of a foreign state or of foreign states had no little influence in determining the position of the government on questions of foreign politics. Conspicuous statesmen were pleased on public occasions to display the orders and decorations which they had received from foreign princes, and in this they did violence to the republican spirit of the people.

"The cantonal constitutions, therefore, in the third decade of this century, forbade, as a rule, not only military capitulations,[1] but also the reception of pensions and titles from foreign states, as also the wearing of foreign orders while in official position."[2] Later provisions of a similar import were embodied in the federal constitution. They were set down in Article 12, as follows: "The members of the federal authorities, the civil and military functionaries of the Union, and the federal representatives or com-

[1] "Une capitulation militaire était un traité conclu avec un gouvernement étranger et par lequel un ou plusieurs cantons suisses s'engageaient à lui fournir, moyennant finance, un certain nombre d'hommes armés." Droz, " Instruction Civique," 167.

[2] Blumer, I, 229.

missioners may receive from a foreign government neither pensions or salaries, nor titles, presents, or decorations.

"If they are already in possession of pensions, titles, or decorations, they must renounce the enjoyment of their pensions and the use of their titles and decorations during their continuance in office.

"Nevertheless the inferior employees may be authorized by the Federal Council to receive their pensions.

"In the federal army, neither decorations nor titles accorded by a foreign government may be borne.

" All officers, subordinate officers, and soldiers, are prohibited from accepting distinctions of this sort."

The prohibition here set forth may be compared with that involved in those clauses of the United States Constitution, which provide that no title of nobility shall be granted either by the United States or by any State, and that "no person holding any office of profit or trust under them shall, without the consent of the Congress, accept of any present, emolument, office, or title, of any kind whatever, from any king, prince, or foreign state."[1]

[1] U. S. Constitution, Art. I, Secs. 9 and 10.

CHAPTER VIII.

INTERNAL RELATIONS.

IN the second article of the federal constitution are enumerated the ends for which the Union exists. The first of these is the maintenance of the nation in a state of independence of foreign powers. Nearly all laws relating to foreign affairs have this as their direct or indirect object. The second end of the Union there specified is the maintenance of peace and order within. Although put in the second place in the article enumerating the purposes of the Union, this end is in some sense a condition of the first; for without internal peace and harmony, the continued independence of the nation would be impossible. The constitutional basis of legislation for the preservation of internal peace and order is set forth in the following provisions of the fourteenth article: "The cantons are bound whenever conflicts arise among them to abstain from taking up arms, and from all independent action in their own behalf, and to subject themselves to the decisions which shall be rendered on these conflicts in accordance with federal prescriptions."

As already indicated, conflicts which arise under the constitution or in connection with the federal decrees and concordats are settled by the Federal Council and the Federal Assembly. Civil conflicts, on the other hand, are judged by the Federal Tribunal.[1] Under Article 61, which provides that "final civil judgments rendered in one canton are executory in the whole of Switzerland," a question sometimes arises as to the obligation of one canton to carry out the decree of the cantonal court of another canton, and this question has to be decided by the federal authorities. An attempt on the part of a court of one canton to execute its decrees in another canton, in the face of the indifference or willful neglect of the second body, is an act prohibited by Article 14. The procedure in such a case is through an application to the federal authorities for a judgment requiring the second canton to fulfill its obligation.

The provisions made by decrees and judicial decisions for the settlement of intercantonal conflicts are inadequate to preserve peace and order, unless supported by other provisions for

[1] Articles 110-113.

the exercise of force to the same end. This fact appears to have been perceived by the makers of the Swiss constitution, and in Article 16 they laid down the rule under which internal order may be enforced. This article provides that "in case of internal disorder, or when danger is threatened by another canton, the government of the canton menaced must inform the Federal Council of the impending danger immediately, in order that this body may be able to take the necessary measures within the limits of its competence,[1] or convoke the Federal Assembly. Whenever there is urgency, the government of the threatened canton is authorized, on immediately informing the Federal Council, to ask aid of other cantons which are obliged to render it. When the government of this canton is not in a condition to ask aid, the competent federal authority *may* intervene without requisition; it *must* do so when the disorders endanger the security of Switzerland."

It is to be observed that by these provisions disturbances of the peace within a canton are subjected to the same remedial measures as attacks of one canton on another. It is to be observed, moreover, that these measures consist in an appeal to the federal government, as the rule, and in an appeal to other cantons as the

[1] These are defined by Art. 102, Secs. 3, 10, and 11.

exception. The development of means of communication by telegraph and railway has made it as easy at the present time for a threatened canton to appeal to the Federal Council as to a neighboring canton, and therefore use is seldom made of the permitted exception. It is now almost exclusively the practice for a canton to demand aid only of the federal government. If this position of a Swiss canton is compared with that of an American State, it will be found that the State is the more independent of external interference. It is not obliged to obey the summons of any other State for help; it has, in fact, no right to render such aid. The federal government in the United States may not interfere to preserve order in a State, except on the request of the legislature or the executive of this State, while in Switzerland a canton must render aid when asked for it by another canton, and the federal government may intervene in the affairs of a canton under certain circumstances, even when the canton has not applied for such intervention. "But the Swiss Union will always, so long as it receives no notice, be obliged to proceed on the presumption that no danger exists or that the respective canton is strong enough to manage its own affairs. A disturbance which the power of the canton is quite competent to control offers no occasion for the intervention of the federal authorities."[1]

In case of federal intervention in the affairs of a canton the federal authorities are enjoined from violating the rights of the cantons, which have been established by the fifth article of the federal constitution. The expenses of such an intervention are borne, as a rule, by the canton which demanded it or occasioned it; but the Federal Assembly may provide that, on account of special circumstances, the expenses shall be paid out of the federal treasury.[2]

In case of actual hostilities arising through the antagonisms of cantons among themselves, or through the unfriendly attitude of foreign powers, every canton is required to permit the free passage of troops over its territory; and it is further provided that these troops shall be under federal command.[3]

The internal relations of a federal union are further illustrated by the laws which fix the attitude of a State towards criminals taking refuge within its territory from another State. An independent state has the power to determine whether the criminal shall be protected in his place of refuge, or expelled beyond the borders,

[1] Rüttimann, "Das nordamerikanische Bundesstaatsrecht verglichen mit den politischen Einrichtungen der Schweiz." II, 81.
[2] Article 16, Secs. 3 and 4.
[3] Article 17.

or handed over to the authorities of the state in which the crime was committed. If it becomes bound to pursue the last-named course, it is by a voluntary agreement entered into with another state or with other states, and such an agreement has only a moral force, there being no power which may legitimately compel its observance. But the action of a member of a federal union in this regard is usually determined by the federal constitution, or by federal legislation had in pursuance of constitutional provisions. In the American Union, the course which a State must pursue is clearly marked out by the federal Constitution: "A person charged in any State with treason, felony, or other crime, who shall flee from justice, and be found in another State, shall, on demand of the executive authority of the State from which he fled, be delivered up, to be removed to the State having jurisdiction of the crime."[1]

This provision extends to both statutory and common-law crimes, but concerns only such persons as have fled from justice, that is to say, "the person accused must have been within the jurisdiction of the State accusing him, and must have fled therefrom. If, in fact, he was never within it, he cannot have fled from its justice; and therefore a person who in another State

[1] Article IV, Sec. 2.

may have conspired with others to commit an offense in Missouri, is not demandable by Missouri as a fugitive. But if he was within the State at the time of committing the offense, he is held to be a fugitive if he left without awaiting the consequences of his conduct."[1] The demand must be based on a charge against the accused made in some due form of law, and when presented it becomes the duty of the executive on whom it is made to respond to it; but if he shall refuse to do so the federal tribunals have no power to compel obedience. "If the State to which an offender has fled has herself against him some unsatisfied demands of justice, it is proper for her to proceed to enforce it before honoring a requisition."[2] If, moreover, there are other charges against the offender besides that on which his extradition is had, he must be allowed to return to the State which has surrendered him before he can be prosecuted on any other charge.

While the Constitution of the United States contains clear and specific provisions for the extradition of offenders, the federal constitution of Switzerland defers the whole matter to federal legislation, setting forth, however, the single limitation that "extradition may not be rendered

[1] Cooley, "General Principles of Constitutional Law," 190.
[2] Cooley, 192.

obligatory for political crimes and those of the press."[1] In view of the marked differences in the political character of the cantons, this limitation appears reasonable, in fact necessary to prevent a canton from sometimes being called upon to do violence to its own convictions by delivering up a political offender whose acts appear rather to merit praise than punishment.

This subject was taken up by federal legislation in the law of July 24, 1852. It was made the duty of every canton to permit the arrest and extradition of those persons who had been condemned for certain crimes or who were accused of such crimes in due legal form. In the United States the law fails to specify the crimes for which extradition may be had, simply adhering to the constitutional designation of "treason, felony, or other crimes;" but in Switzerland the second article of the law of 1852 enumerates the crimes for which one canton may demand from another the extradition of the criminal.[2] As an exception to the general rule,

[1] Article 55 of the Constitution of 1848, and Article 67 of that of 1874.

[2] They are: "Mord, Kindsmord, Todtschlag und Tödtung durch Fahrlässigkeit; Abtreibung und Aussetzung, Brandstiftung, Raub, Erpressung, Diebstahl, Unterschlagung, Pfanddefraudation, Betrug, betrüglicher Bankerott, böswillige Eigenthumsschädigung mit Ausnahme unbedeutender Fälle; schwere Körperverletzung, Nothzucht, Blutschande, widernatürliche

extradition may be refused, of persons who have acquired citizenship, or who have settled in a canton, when this canton binds itself to try and punish them according to its own laws, or allows a sentence already pronounced to be executed. This provision, which is wanting in both Germany and the United States, establishes an international relation rather than a relation befitting members of a federal state. If a person is accused of several crimes committed in different cantons, he shall be handed over to all the cantons in order, first to that canton in which the gravest crime was committed. If, moreover, one crime is committed in several cantons, that canton in which the principal action was had may demand the extradition of all those who have been guilty of participation in the offense in other cantons.

It has been found expedient to bring the members of a federal union into some clearly defined legal relation to one another, not only with respect to criminal affairs, but also with respect to civil cases. In this regard the cantons

Wollust (Sodomie), Bigamie, Menschenraub, Entführung, Unterdrückung des Familienstandes, Anmassung eines fremden Familienstandes, Bestechung, Missbrauch der Amtsgewalt, Anmassung der Amtsgewalt, Fälschung, Meineid, falsches Zeugniss, falsche Verzeigung in Bezug auf die hier bezeichneten Vergehen, Münzfälschung oder andere dazu gehörende Vergehen.'' Blumer, I, 255.

of Switzerland hold a somewhat more intimate relation to one another than the States of the American Union. As already noticed, final civil judgments rendered in one canton are executory in any other canton. No such latitude as this is given to a decision of a State court in the United States. The Constitution provides, however, that "full faith and credit shall be given in each State to the public acts, records, and judicial proceedings of every other State. And the Congress may by general laws prescribe the manner in which such acts, records, and proceedings shall be proved, and the effect thereof."[1] In pursuance of the provisions of the last sentence of this section, the Congress has provided that "the acts of the legislature of any State or Territory, or of any country subject to the jurisdiction of the United States, shall be authenticated by having the seals of such Territory, State, or country affixed thereto. The records and judicial proceedings of the courts of any State or Territory, or of any country, shall be proved or admitted in any other court within the United States, by the attestation of the clerk, and the seal of the court annexed, if there be a seal, together with a certificate of the judge, chief justice, or presiding magistrate, that the said attestation is in due form. And the said rec-

[1] Article 4, Sec. 1.

ords and judicial proceedings, so authenticated, shall have such faith and credit given to them in every court within the United States as they have by law or usage in the courts of the State from which they are taken."[1]

These provisions regarding the weight to be given to the public acts and records of one State in another State appear important in view of the impossibility of enforcing a civil judgment by a State court except in the State where it is rendered. If it becomes necessary to enforce such a judgment outside of these limits, the end can be reached only by a new action in the second State, demanded on the ground of the former judgment and supported by the records and proceedings of the former trial. In a similar case in Switzerland, however, no new trial is required, the way being open to an immediate execution of the judgment either in the canton where it was rendered or in any other canton.

[1] Revised Statutes of the United States (1878), § 905.

CHAPTER IX.

THE ARMY AND THE FINANCES.

IN establishing constitutional provisions with respect to the army, the Swiss have been careful to avoid the danger to liberty which a prominent development of military affairs would present. In the early history of the Confederation the several cantons were dissuaded from maintaining permanent military forces by the economical burdens which the support of such forces would impose. The Helvetic Republic, in alliance with France, was, however, obliged to maintain a standing army. "The Act of Mediation, which gave the Union no financial means for paying regular troops, took care that the cantons should not win too strong a position in opposition to the federal power, and to this end limited the number of paid troops which a canton might maintain, to two hundred men."[1] With the adoption of the articles of confera-

[1] Blumer, II, 315.

tion, of 1815, there was a return towards the ancient independence of the cantons, and the limitation which had been imposed on the military power of the cantons by the Act of Mediation, was removed. In the project for revising the constitution, which was brought forward in 1832, it was proposed so to restrict the power of the individual canton in this regard, that, without the consent of the federal authorities, it might not maintain more than three hundred men as a standing force. Essentially the same restriction appeared also in the constitution of 1848, where it was provided that no canton or half-canton should, without the consent of the federal authorities, maintain a standing force of more than three hundred men, not including the *Landjägerkorps*. And this provision of 1848 was retained in the amended constitution of 1874.[1] But the practice of the cantons has fallen so far within these legal limitations, that at present no canton maintains any standing troops whatsoever. The federal government, however, maintains military schools, in which a large number of persons are almost constantly under instruction, but these do not constitute a standing army, and therefore the conduct of the federal authorities in this matter is not in conflict with the prohibition of Article 13 of the present constitution.

[1] Article 13.

THE ARMY AND THE FINANCES. 191

Inasmuch as the existence of any government presumes the capacity to exercise force, it is clear that, in case of a constitutional provision prohibiting the maintenance of a standing army, there must be some legal means provided through which, in case of need, an army may be called into active existence. The federal government of Switzerland has solved this problem by making every Swiss liable to military service. It provides, moreover, for furnishing, when required, support to those who have suffered a permanent loss of health in this service, or to the families of those who have lost their lives. The law embracing these provisions also ordains that soldiers entering the service of the Federation shall receive, without charge, their first equipment, clothing, and arms; and, moreover, that they shall retain their arms under conditions established by the federal legislature. The same authority shall also fix the conditions of the tax for exemption from military service.

The military organization as existing at present is the result of a long period of growth, and many of its features may be traced through the successive fundamental laws of Switzerland. The basis of the existing organization, which has been perfected through federal legislation, is found in the following articles of the constitution of 1874 :—

"Article 19. The federal army is composed : (*a*) Of the regular troops of the cantons; (*b*) of all citizens who, not belonging to these troops, are nevertheless liable to military service.

"The control of the army as well as of the munitions of war provided by law belongs to the Federation.

"In case of danger, the Federation has also the right of direct and exclusive control over men not incorporated in the federal army and all the other military resources of the cantons.

"The cantons control the military forces of their territory, in so far as this right is not limited by federal laws or the constitution.

"Article 20. Laws relating to the organization of the army emanate from the Federation. The military laws in the cantons are executed within the limits prescribed by federal legislation and under the surveillance of the Federation, by means of the cantonal authority.

"It belongs to the Federation to provide arms and all military instruction.

"It belongs to the cantons to furnish and maintain the clothing and equipment. The cantons are, however, reimbursed for the expense, in accordance with rules established by federal legislation.

THE ARMY AND THE FINANCES. 193

"Article 21. In so far as it is not in opposition to military considerations the several corps should be formed from soldiers from the same canton.

" The composition of these corps, the care of maintaining their effectiveness, the nomination and promotion of their officers, belong to the cantons, under the limitations of the general prescriptions which are sent to them by the Federation.

"Article 22. For an equitable indemnity, the Federation may use or purchase all arsenals and buildings with their belongings intended for military purposes.

" The conditions of the indemnity shall be regulated by federal legislation."

Since the adoption of these constitutional provisions, the federal legislature has established the details of the military organization. From these provisions it is seen that the military system as a whole has fallen under the authority of the Union. The cantons have to do only with the formation of the several corps, and even here their activity is determined by regulations proceeding from the Federation. Yet under these regulations the functions of the cantons are important. At the expense of the Federation, they care for the clothing and equipment of the troops, and exercise control over their own troops, in so far as their power in this regard is not limited by the federal constitution and laws. The regular federal troops or *Bundesauszug* consists of those liable to military duty between twenty and thirty two years of age, of which, in January, 1887, there were 120,-393. The *Landwehr* embraces those between the ages of thirty-two and forty-five, numbering about 82,000. By a law which went into force in 1887 the *Landsturm* was organized, and made to consist of retired officers under fifty-five years of age, retired non-commissioned officers and privates under fifty, and all between forty and fifty who are not in the *Landwehr*, as well as all able-bodied young men between seventeen and twenty. It is supposed that the *Landsturm* will add about 300,000 men to the effective force of the republic.

In order that the Federation may make use of this force and support the political organization, it must be provided with a revenue. This, according to the constitution, is derived from federal property, from customs duties, from the post and the telegraph, from a monopoly in making and selling powder, from half of the gross product of the tax for military exemptions collected by the cantons, and from the contributions of the cantons, which are regulated by federal legislation, with special reference to the wealth and taxable property of the cantons. The first item in the list of sources, namely, federal property, represents no real source of income, inasmuch as any return which it may yield is more than offset by the interest on the federal debt of 36,670,616 francs. From the customs duties is derived the main support. It was estimated that of the 52,527,000 francs demanded for the budget for 1887, the customs duties and postal-telegraph service would yield 44,435,200 francs.

In the government monopoly of the manufacture of gunpowder,[1] the Federation has shown a determination to engage directly in the business of production. The same determination is shown also in the constitutional amendment of October 25, 1885, and the legislation had under the provisions of this amendment. By this amendment the Federation is authorized to make provision, by law, concerning the manufacture and sale of distilled liquors. " The net revenues derived from the taxation of the sale of distilled liquors accrue to the cantons in which the liquors are sold. The net revenues of the Federation, derived from the inland manufacture and from the corresponding duties upon the importation of distilled liquors, are distributed among all the cantons in proportion to their

[1] Swiss Federal Constitution, Art. 41.

population. Of these revenues the cantons must devote at least ten per cent to the suppression of alcoholism."

Under the provisions of this constitutional amendment, was passed the Spirit Monopoly Bill of 1886. This bill, having passed the Federal Assembly, was submitted to a popular vote on the petition of 48,255 citizens. The popular vote confirmed the law, which provides, in substance, as follows :—

"The Federation has the exclusive right to manufacture and import distilled liquors. Approximately a quarter of the necessary supply is obtained by contracts with inland producers. The distilled liquors are sold for cash by the Federation in quantities of at least 150 litres. The price is fixed from time to time by the Federal Council. It shall not amount to less than 120 francs nor more than 150 francs per hectolitre of pure alcohol.[1] The sale of distilled liquors in quantities of at least forty litres is a business free to all; but trade in smaller quantities is subject to a license on the part of the cantonal authorities, and must pay to the cantons, according to the amount of the transactions, a tax on sales, fixed by the cantons until the

[1] "Denaturalized spirits, that is, alcohol so treated as to prevent its use in the manufacture of beverages, are sold at cost price for technical and household purposes."

passage of a federal law. The net profits of the administration of the federal monopoly are divided among the several cantons in proportion to the population."[1] In many other departments of production the direct agency of the Federation is manifest, but none of these undertakings is important as a source of revenue. From the monopoly of the manufacture and sale of gunpowder there is realized about 500,000 francs annually.

The military tax is imposed upon every Swiss citizen of the age of military liability, living within or without the territory of the Federation, and who does not personally perform military service. "Foreigners established in Switzerland are likewise subject to this tax, unless they are exempt therefrom by virtue of international treaties or belong to a state in which the Swiss are neither liable to military service nor to the payment of any equivalent tax in money." The following classes of persons are exempt :—

"1. Paupers assisted by the public charity fund; and those who by reason of mental or physical infirmity are incapable of earning their subsistence, or who have not a sufficient fortune for the support of themselves and family.

[1] See *Political Science Quarterly*, March, 1889, p. 59, article by Gustav Cohn, on "Income and Property Taxes in Switzerland."

"2. Those rendered unfit through previous service.

"3. Swiss citizens in foreign countries, if they are subject to a personal service, or to an exemption tax for the same in place of domicils.

"4. The railway and steamboat employees during the time when they are liable to the military service organized for the working of the railways and steamboats in time of war.

"5. Policemen and the federal frontier guards.

"The military tax consists in a personal tax of six francs and of an additional tax on property and income, the amount exacted from any one taxpayer not to exceed 3,000 francs per annum." The additional tax is one franc and a half for each one thousand francs of net fortune, and one franc and a half for each one hundred francs of net income. Net fortunes less than one thousand francs are exempt, and from the net income there is to be deducted six hundred francs. Net fortune is the personal and real property after deducting debts of record, chattels necessary for household, tools of trade, and agricultural implements. Real estate and improvements are assessed at three-fourths of the market value.

"In computing the property of a person for this tax, half of the fortune of the parents, or, if not living, then of the grandparents, is included proportionally to number of children or grandchildren, unless the father of the taxpayer shall himself perform military service or pay the exemption tax.

"Net income embraces: 1. The earnings of an art, profession, trade, business, occupation, or employment. The expenses incurred to obtain these earnings are deducted, also necessary household expenses, and five per cent of the capital invested in a business. 2. The product of annuities, pensions, and other similar revenues.

"From the age of thirty-three to the completion of the military age only one-half of the tax is exacted.

"The Federal Assembly has the right to increase the tax to double the amount for those years in which the greater part of the elite troops (as distinguished from the *Landwehr* or reserve) are called into active service.

"The military tax for Swiss citizens residing abroad is calculated every year by special rolls and the persons advised by the officials of the canton of their birth. The tax for exemption is paid in the canton where the taxpayer is domiciled when the rolls are prepared. Parents are responsible for the payment of the tax for their minor sons and for those sons who, though of age, remain a part of their household.

"The period for prescription is five years for taxpayers present in the country and ten years for those absent from the country. The cantons are charged with making out the annual rolls and collecting the tax. By the end of January following the year of the tax the cantons must remit to the Federation the half of the net product collected, a portion of which is assigned by the Federal Assembly to the fund for military pensions.

"The estimated receipts from this tax for the share of the Federation is placed in the budget for the year 1887 at 1,235,000 francs."

The military exemption law has not been accepted without opposition. Dr. Dubs has criticised it very sharply. "The conception of this law," he says, "is really unworthy of acceptance. If the constitutional principle of the general liability to military service were in fact carried out, such a law would naturally have no sense, and would at most be a tax on mental and physical infirmity, that is to say, a tax which must be characterized as almost shameful. The whole law has thus its basis only in an improper carrying out of the constitution. With a more correct carrying out of the constitution there would remain only taxation of those absent. But those who are away from home in other parts of Switzerland are now held there to military service, and those outside of Switzerland might at any time be required to return, in order

THE ARMY AND THE FINANCES. 201

to perform their military service in person; but, according to all other principles of our law of taxation, we cannot properly speak of a right to tax those in foreign countries. The law in question is therefore in all points equally irrational, and, in the construction of its details, leads moreover to further absurdities of all kinds, of which undoubtedly the taxation of the heir's possible expectations forms the highest point."[1]

Besides the taxes already mentioned, the Federation may collect a fee of thirty-five francs from foreigners for granting them the right to acquire cantonal and communal citizenship. The Federal Council may also "levy on railway companies a tax of fifty francs for each kilometer in active service, whenever the business of the company shows a net profit after providing a suitable sinking fund of four per cent. Should the profits exceed four per cent., the tax may be increased to a maximum of two hundred francs." The Federation may, moreover, collect from banks one per cent of the amount of their issue; also certain fees for registering trade-marks and commercial houses.[2]

In case the income from these taxes shall prove to be inadequate to federal needs, the

[1] Dubs, II, 230.
[2] "Reports from the Consuls of the United States," Washington, 1888, pp. 618-620.

Federation may have recourse to contributions in money by the cantons, which are provided for by the last clause of Article 42. These contributions were fixed, for twenty years, by the law of October 7, 1874. In assigning the amounts the several cantons shall pay, regard was had to the wealth and population of the cantons. They were divided into eight classes, which might be required to pay 10, 15, 20, 30, 40, 50, 70, and 90 centimes per head of the population. Hitherto it has not been necessary for the Federation to resort to these contributions.

CHAPTER X.

RIGHTS AND PRIVILEGES.

A THIRD aim of the Swiss federal constitution is defined in Article 2, as the protection of the liberty and rights of the citizens. Under the pre-revolutionary confederation, certain towns and districts held a subject relation to the confederated cantons, but this condition of things was set aside by the Revolution, and the Act of Mediation provided that in Switzerland there should be neither subject districts nor privileges of place, birth, persons, or families.[1] In the reactionary movement after 1814, certain political privileges were conceded to important cities and even to distinguished families; and the articles of alliance of 1815 showed a departure from the principles of strict democratic equality which had been embodied in the Act of Mediation. According to the seventh section of these articles

[1] "Il n'y a plus en Suisse ni pays sujets, ni priviliges de lieux, de naissance, de personnes, ou de familles." Act of Mediation, Art. 3.

"the Confederation embraces the principle, that as since the recognition of the twenty-two cantons there are no longer subject lands in Switzerland, so also the enjoyment of political rights can never be the exclusive privilege of a class of the citizens of a canton." This is clearly a less strong and definite statement than that of the previous constitution which it supplants.

The movement of 1830 emphasized once more the principle of political equality, and prepared the way for the revolution of 1848. The federal constitution adopted in this latter year declared: "All Swiss are equal before the law. There are in Switzerland neither subjects, nor privileges of place, birth, persons, or families." (Article 4.) This article passed without amendment into the constitution of 1874. The statement of the principle of equality which it contains is more easily made than the application of it to actual affairs. There are at least two different views regarding its execution. "In its decisions the Federal Council has always proceeded with the view that equality before the law could not be demanded in an absolute but only in a relative sense, that is to say, under the presupposition of entirely equal actual relations." In a decision rendered Nov. 29, 1865, the Council affirmed that "the fourth article of the federal constitution has never been conceived in the sense of an absolute equality of all citizens, and, moreover, cannot be so construed, because the difference of actual and legal relations always produces inequalities. . . . It is, therefore, only demanded that all citizens similarly situated shall be treated alike and not exceptionally."[1]

In apposition to this view, Rüttimann urges that "there is no privilege, in excusing which it may not be affirmed, that under similar actual conditions everyone would participate in it. The exception, that in unequal actual relations legal equality cannot be demanded, would thus completely abolish the rule."[2] He held, moreover, that Article 4 referred to equality of legal capacity; that men were by nature equal, were equally capacitated by birth to acquire every private right and to fill every public position.[3]

Under the earliest constitutions the rights and duties of individual citizens were conceived with reference to other citizens of the same canton. Later legislation, however, has aimed to extend the limits within which equality should prevail. Important in this regard is the forty-eighth article of the constitution of 1848, reproduced as Article 60 of the present constitution

[1] Rüttimann, II, 139.
[2] Rüttimann, II, 140.
[3] Rüttimann, II, 140.

which obliges every canton to treat the citizens of other cantons like its own citizens, in all legislative and judicial matters.[1] This was an indication of a tendency to set aside the ancient particularism, and it opened the way to broader sympathies and the growth of a national spirit. The Swiss had before them in this matter the good example of the United States, where it had already been constitutionally provided that "the citizens of each State shall be entitled to all privileges and immunities of citizens in the several States."[2] A similar doctrine was more definitely set forth later in the imperial constitution of Germany. According to Article 3, "there is one citizenship for all Germany, and the citizens or subjects of each State of the Federation shall be treated in every other State thereof as natives, and shall have the right of becoming permanent residents, of carrying on business, of filling public offices, of acquiring real estate and citizenship of the several States, and may acquire all civil rights on the same conditions as those born in the State, and shall also have the same usage as regards civil prosecutions and the protection of the laws."

[1] "Tous les Cantons sont obligés de traiter les citoyens des autres Etats confédérés comme ceux de leur Etat en motière de législation et pour tout ce qui concerne les voies juridiques." Article 60.

[2] U. S. Constitution, Art. 4, Sec. 2.

The liberal manner in which the several cantons at present treat a citizen of another canton is in marked contrast with that of earlier centuries, when the citizen of any canton was regarded and treated as a foreigner in any other canton. Under the Act of Mediation the citizen of any canton might take up his residence in another canton, and acquire there political rights; but he could not enjoy political rights in two cantons at the same time. The constitution of 1815, however, left each canton free to determine for itself the conditions under which persons from without could settle and gain citizenship. With the adoption of the constitution of 1848, a general law governing this matter was established, which with certain modifications has been retained in the existing constitution. It provides that every Swiss citizen has the right to settle anywhere within the limits of Swiss territory, on condition of producing a certificate of former residence. But the right of settlement may be refused or withdrawn from those who, in consequence of a penal judgment, are no longer in the enjoyment of their civil rights. It may, moreover, be withdrawn from those who have been repeatedly punished for grave offenses, as also from those who have come to depend permanently on public charity for their support.

Citizenship in Switzerland is primarily an

affair of the commune, from which is developed citizenship in the canton. Through this latter we reach the broader conception of citizenship in the Federation. This last follows as a legal consequence of citizenship in a canton, for "every citizen of a canton is a Swiss citizen."[1] The lines of distinction between these several conceptions are, however, not clearly presented even to the minds of the Swiss themselves. The want of clearness is owing in part to the presence of a double conception embracing the view of passive citizenship, in which the subject is maintained in the enjoyment of certain civil rights, and that of active citizenship, under which the subject is endowed with certain political privileges. To quote from a Swiss writer, "the national citizenship proceeds from below; political active citizenship is derived from above, proceeding from the Federation and from this source descending to the canton and the commune of residence."[2] The Swiss citizen, having shown his right of suffrage, may take part, in the place where he has acquired a residence, in all votes and elections concerning federal af-

[1] Article 43; "Der Besitz des schwiezerischen Bürgerrechtes hängt von demjenigen eines Kantonsbürgerrechtes ab, wie letzterer hinwieder in der Regel denjenigen eeies Gemeindsbürgerrechtes vorausetzt." Blumer, I, 330.

[2] Dubs, "Das Oeffentliche Recht der schweizerischen Eidgenossenschaft," II, 11.

fairs; but he cannot exercise political rights in more than one canton. Coming from any part of the Federation and taking up his residence in any canton, he enjoys in his place of settlement all the rights of a citizen of the canton, and with these also all the rights of a citizen of the commune. He is, however, excluded from participating in the common property of the citizens and the corporations, as well as from voting on purely municipal affairs, unless it has been otherwise decided by cantonal legislation. He obtains the right of voting on cantonal and municipal affairs after a residence of three months. This is a material limitation of the period of residence previously required for this purpose. Under the constitution of 1848, there might be required of Swiss citizens settling in a canton a residence of two years as a condition of voting on cantonal affairs, and they were entirely excluded from the right of voting on the affairs of a commune. In order that no limitations of this extended liberty may be made through cantonal legislation without the consent of the supreme authority, it is provided that cantonal laws concerning settlement and the electoral rights which citizens acquiring residence in a canton may enjoy in communal affairs must be submitted for the sanction of the Federal Council.[1]

[1] Article 43.

With respect to civil rights, settlers in any canton stand, as a rule, under the laws of their place of residence. The application of this law is under the direction of the federal authorities, through which also measures are taken to prevent the same property or income from being taxed in two cantons at the same time.[1]

By Article 48 it is decreed that a federal law shall establish provisions respecting the care and burial of poor inhabitants of one canton, who have fallen sick or died in another canton. The federal law called for in this article was passed in June, 1875. It ordered that the authorities of the place in which the sickness or the death occurred should provide care for the sick and burial for the dead without being allowed to demand compensation from the home canton of the victim.[2]

It is noteworthy that Swiss citizenship once held is much less easily lost or set aside than that of most other nations. In this matter the federal constitution determines the conduct of the cantons. In order to prevent the increase of the unsettled class, the constitution of 1848 interdicted a canton from depriving a citizen of his citizenship. This provision is strengthened in Article 44 of the present constitution, where

[1] Article 46.
[2] Von Orelli, p. 70.

it is declared that no canton may banish one of its citizens from its territory, or deprive him of his citizenship. "Federal legislation shall determine the conditions under which foreigners may be naturalized, as also those under which a Swiss may renounce his citizenship in order to obtain naturalization in a foreign country."[1] The doctrine of the laws that have been enacted on this point as interpreted by the Federal Council has been summed up as follows: " Swiss citizenship is imprescriptible; every Swiss retains his citizenship as long as he himself does not renounce it, and as long as its legally valid derivation can be shown. The mere fact of the acquisition of citizenship in a foreign state is not adequate to cause the loss of citizenship of a canton which one enjoys; nor is adequate to this end a long absence in a foreign country, even when the person concerned has neither fulfilled his military duty nor paid taxes; nor, moreover, the entrance into foreign civil or military service. Rather for the loss of cantonal citizenship there is required a formal and express voluntary declaration. This declaration is then valid for all minor children. But in order to make a valid renunciation of citizenship of a canton, proof of the acquisition of citizen-

[1] Article 44.

ship in another state or canton must be furnished."[1]

Conspicuous among the rights and privileges that have been acquired by the Swiss is the right of worshiping in any manner approved by the conscience of the worshiper. The progress of enlightenment in Switzerland which this privilege represents is fully appreciated only when viewed in contrast with the ecclesiastical narrowness and sectarian antagonisms of earlier centuries. It is, moreover, one of the later achievements in liberty. As late as the war of the Sonderbund, religious intolerance appeared to threaten the integrity of the Confederation; and under the constitution of 1848 toleration was extended to only two sects, the Roman Catholic and the Reformed. Through the constitution of 1874, however, a far more liberal attitude was assumed. In Articles 49 to 52 inclusive are set forth the foundations of religious liberty in so far as this has been achieved in Switzerland.

[1] Blumer, I, 333. In 1885 "the Federal Council refused to conclude a treaty of reciprocal naturalization with the United States of America, because of the clause stipulating that the Swiss who should obtain the rights of Americans, should lose their primitive rights as Swiss. This is contrary to the Swiss constitution, which declares that no Swiss citizen, unless he fights against his country, can ever lose his original rights." —*Annual Register 1885, p. 286.*

RIGHTS AND PRIVILEGES. 213

"Liberty of belief and conscience is inviolable. No one can be forced to take part in a religious association, to follow a religious teaching, to perform a religious act, or to undergo penalties of any kind whatsoever, on account of religious opinion. The person who exercises paternal or tutelary authority has the right to determine the religious education of the children, in accordance with the foregoing principles, until the age of sixteen years. The exercise of civil or political rights cannot be limited by any prescriptions or conditions whatsoever of a religious or ecclesiastical nature. No one on account of religious opinion is released from the performance of civil duties. No one is required to pay taxes which are specially devoted to the peculiar expenses of the worship of a religious community to which he does not belong. The final execution of this principle is reserved to federal legislation.

"Freedom of worship is guaranteed within limits compatible with public order and good morals. The cantons and the Federation may take such measures as are necessary to preserve public order and peace among the members of the different religious communities; as also against the encroachments of the ecclesiastical authorities upon the rights of the citizens or of the state. Contests under public or private law arising from the creation of religious communities, or from the separation of religious communities already existing, may be taken for decision before the competent federal authorities. Bishoprics may not be created on Swiss territory without the consent of the Federation.

"The order of Jesuits and the societies affiliated with them cannot be admitted into any part of Switzerland, and all activity in the church and school is prohibited to their members. This interdiction may also be extended, by way of federal decree, to other religious orders, whose activity is dangerous to the state, or disturbs the peace among the sects.

"It is prohibited to found new convents or religious orders, and to re-establish those which have been suppressed."

Under the old order of things, while the cantons controlled the legislation respecting marriage, the liberty of individual citizens in this regard was limited by property, residence, and religious conditions. At present, however, "the right of marriage stands under the protection of the Federation. No obstacle to marriage can be based upon religious motives, upon the indigence of one party or the other, upon their previous conduct, or upon any other motive whatsoever recognizable by the police. A marriage concluded in any canton or in a foreign country, in accordance with the laws there in force, will be recognized as valid throughout the Federation. A woman acquires by marriage the residence rights of her husband. Children born before marriage are rendered legitimate by the subsequent marriage of their parents."[1] Certain fees or taxes that were previously imposed upon the contracting parties are, by the present constitution, made illegal. Legislation under these constitutional provisions was had December 24, 1874. Among other things, it established the details of the conditions under which marriages might be contracted, and also the conditions under which marriages might be declared void and divorces granted.[2] By making marriage and divorce subjects of federal rather than of State legislation, Switzerland has taken a step in advance of the position at present occupied by the United States.

The views of the Swiss at different times with respect to the liberty of the press show the growth of a sentiment favorable to the enlargement of federal authority. In the projected constitutional reform of 1833, it was proposed that the press should stand entirely under cantonal legislation, and the Union should be able neither to abolish nor to limit its freedom, nor to

[1] Article 54.
[2] Blumer, I, 381–391.

introduce a censorship of the press. "In the commission of 1848 for the revision of the constitution it was at once recognized that this provision was insufficient; it was seen to be needed, on the one hand, that the freedom of the press should be guaranteed by the Union; on the other hand, that the Union should have the right to take action in opposition to abuses directed against itself."[1] The outcome of the discussion was the formation of Article 45, of the constitution of 1848, which is retained unchanged in the existing constitution: "The freedom of the press is guaranteed. With reference to the abuse of this freedom, the cantonal legislation shall embrace the necessary provisions, which, however, require the approval of the Federal Council. The Federation has the right to establish penalties to repress the abuses of the liberty of publication, which are directed against itself or its authorities."[2]

Under this law it is not permitted to establish a preliminary censorship; to subject the press to administrative discretion; to make an exception, to the disadvantage of the press, to the generally accepted penal rules; to set up for the crimes of the press another court than that of the place of publication or of the residence of the accused;

[1] Blumer, I, 391.
[2] Article 55.

or to suppress completely a newspaper or other periodical.[1] It is, moreover, to be observed that cantonal laws with reference to the press are not operative until they have received the sanction of the Federal Council, a provision which is not universally approved among Swiss publicists. It is held by some that it would be a better arrangement for controlling the press, if the whole matter were placed directly under the authorities of the Union.

The freedom of the press is scarcely more important for the achievement and maintenance of political liberty than the right to form associations. Of this latter topic it was at first proposed to make no mention in the constitution of 1848. Through the influence of Zurich and Luzern, however, it was finally determined to guarantee this right under certain limitations. To this end, therefore, was formulated Article 46, of the constitution of 1848, which was retained as Article 56, of the constitution of 1874. It decrees that "the citizens have the right to form associations, provided there is nothing illegal, or dangerous to the state, in the end of these associations or in the means which they employ."[2] It decrees, moreover, that whatever measures are necessary for the repression of abuses un-

[1] Von Orelli, 72.
[2] Article 56.

der this right shall be provided by cantonal legislation. In commenting on this article, Blumer emphasizes the fact that the constitution does not guarantee an absolute right of forming associations any more than absolute freedom of the press. The evident design here was to impose greater restrictions than were laid on the press, in fact, to prohibit at once all associations "whose existence and activity appear incompatible with political order."[1] It is to be observed, moreover, that the right of association is guaranteed only to Swiss citizens, and not to foreigners residing in Switzerland. In imposing penalties the cantons exercise in respect to associations more extensive powers than with respect to the press; for the penal laws of the cantons concerning associations do not require federal sanction in order to become operative. The principle of this act, however, does not permit all cantons to exclude arbitrarily all associations from their territories, and thus defeat the intention of the law. In contrast to the liberty of the press and of association, the right of petition is guaranteed without limitation.

It has been properly regarded as one of the privileges of a free citizen that he should not be tried except before the court of his place of residence. In keeping with this idea the federal

[1] Blumer, I, 403.

constitution has provided that "the solvent debtor who has a fixed residence in Switzerland must be tried on account of personal claims before the judge of his place of residence, and therefore his property cannot be seized or sequestered outside of the canton where he lives, for the satisfaction of personal claims." Article 58 carries the judicial restrictions still further, and provides that "no one shall be withdrawn from his constitutional judge," or, as stated in the French text, "from his natural judge." By this it is proposed to regulate the judicial affairs within the several cantons. In the cantonal constitutions the competence of the judicial officers is usually defined, and "for every inhabitant of the canton the court is determined under whose jurisdiction he stands in both civil and criminal matters."[1] The constitutional judge is, therefore, the one provided by the terms of the judicial constitution, and an exceptional court is one created after the appearance of the case to be judged.[2] It is, then, the purpose of the federal constitution, in the first place, to provide against the arbitrary removal of cases from those courts where they "naturally" or "constitutionally" belong; in the second place, to increase the security of the accused by

[1] Blumer, I, 445.
[2] Von Orelli, 73.

the constitutional prohibition of the introduction of exceptional courts. The first clause of this article (58) is a reproduction of Article 53, of the constitution of 1848, with a single verbal change. The second clause, however, abolishing ecclesiastical jurisdiction, appears first in the constitution as amended in 1874.[1]

Prior to 1848 the penal legislation of Switzerland was in the hands of the cantons. The federal constitution adopted in that year made the first limitation on the power of the cantons in this regard. It ordered that no death sentence should be pronounced on account of political crimes. In the constitutional revision of 1874, it was proposed, in the first place, to make this prohibition general, and, in the second place, to forbid the confiscation of property on account of political offenses. The second proposition was rejected; but the first, providing for the complete abolition of capital punishment, was adopted, and became the first clause of Article 65. This article decreed, moreover, (1) that in time of war the provisions of the military penal code should remain intact; (2) that corporal punishment should be prohibited. This was evidently a benevolent experiment in legislation on the part of the Federation; but at the

[1] The clause here referred to is : "La juridiction ecclésiastique est abolie."

same time it was an unwarrantable interference in the affairs of the cantons. The death penalty was abolished, but no adequate substitute was provided, and subsequent events failed to justify this extreme liberality. In 1879, therefore, this article was again modified. It was made to prohibit capital punishment for political offenses, and corporal punishment under all circumstances; but it left the several cantons free to reintroduce the death penalty for other than political crimes, and this several of them have already done.

One of the results of the early Swiss unions was the establishment of free trade between the districts or cities united. The Act of Mediation guaranteed "la libre circulation des denrées, bestiaux et marchandises;" and the alliance of 1815 provided for like freedom with respect to provisions, products of the soil, and the wares of merchants, and also that these articles and cattle might be freely exported or transported from one canton to another, subject only to proper police regulations.[1] In the constitution of 1848 these provisions from 1815 were reproduced subject to certain reservations:—

1. The royalty on the purchase and sale of powder and salt.

2. Police regulations of the cantons with re-

[1] Article 11.

spect to the carrying on of trade and industry, and the use of the roads.

3. Regulations against injurious forestalling.

4. Transitory sanitary-police regulations in case of epidemic diseases.

5. Dues imposed or recognized by the Diet, which the Union has not abolished.

6. The tax on the consumption of wine and other alcoholic drinks, provided for by a subsequent article of the constitution.

The regulations referred to under 1 and 2 were to affect alike the citizens of the different cantons, and before they could be lawfully carried out they had to be laid before the Federal Council and receive its approbation.

The provisions here set forth and interpreted by the later action of the federal authorities were, in all essential particulars, embodied in the constitution of 1874; the freedom of trade and industry was guaranteed throughout the extent of the Federation; and the regulations involved in the reservations were not permitted to interfere with the principle of commercial and industrial freedom. According to Article 33, of the present constitution, however, it remained for the cantons to make the exercise of the liberal professions dependent on the proof of qualification; but at the same time it devolved upon the Union to make these proofs of qualification valid for the whole Federation.

"Besides the fundamental rights of Swiss citizens established by the federal constitution, the Federation guarantees also all political and individual rights which exist under the cantonal constitutions. The latter and the rights of the nation and individual citizens derived from them, as also the authority of the officers, stand, according to Article 5,[1] under the powerful protection of the Federation. According to the seventh clause of Article 85, regulations which have as their purpose to guarantee the cantonal constitutions fall within the jurisdiction of the Federal Assembly, and according to the third clause of Article 102, it remains with the Federal Council to supervise this guarantee. On the first occasion which presented itself, the Federal Council issued the following statement regarding the position which the federal authorities have to assume with respect to complaints made to them:—

"When complaints are made regarding the violation of the constitution in a canton, and these are brought before the federal authorities,

[1] "La Confédération garantit anx cantons leur territoire, leur souveraineté dans les limites fixées par l'article 3, leurs constitutions, la liberté et les droits du peuple, les droits constitutionnels des citoyens, ainsi que les droits et les attributions que le peuple a conférés aux autorités." Art. 5.

the latter become in duty bound to investigate them and to form a decision as to their foundation or want of foundation, and as to necessary further regulations. For the Federation guarantees the constitutional rights of the citizen as well as the rights of the authorities. The earlier articles of union also guaranteed the constitutions, but this guarantee was otherwise explained, and many complaints of unconstitutional proceedings and circumstances were raised and disregarded. It was desired that these should be no longer endured, and there was demanded an effective guarantee against violations of the constitutions. Thus arose Article 5, of the federal constitution, which guaranteed with an almost pedantic care the rights of the nation and the constitutional rights of the citizens. It would, in fact, be a remarkable relapse into the old view and order of things, a striking denial of the principle contained in Article 5, if we were to assume that, in case of a formally presented complaint, the federal authorities were free to interfere or not. We hold rather that in such cases the federal authorities are obliged to take up the complaints and render a decision regarding them."[1]

The consideration of the specific rights and privileges which exist under the cantonal constitutions and are thus guaranteed by federal au-

[1] Blumer, I, 469-470.

thority belongs to the study of these constitutions, in other words, to the study of local government in Switzerland.

CHAPTER XI.

THE COMMON PROSPERITY.

IN the second article of the federal constitution, which enumerates the aims of the Federation, the fourth aim specified is the promotion of the common prosperity. In pursuing this comprehensive purpose, it has been found necessary not merely to create institutions, but also to set aside certain of those already in existence. Conspicuous among the regulations that had to be set aside in order to secure the end in view, were the restrictions which had been placed by the cantons on intercantonal trade. By the constitution of 1848 the control of the tariff system was transferred to the Union, which was empowered to make all necessary provisions for collecting import, export, and transit duties. Certain sums collected were to be distributed to the several cantons as compensation for the cantonal dues which by the adoption of this constitution and subsequent legislation were revoked. All sums over and above what was required to compensate the cantons were turned into the federal treasury. Although the cantons were deprived of the power to impose tariffs or tolls, yet the Federation might grant them the privilege to levy and collect tolls to promote the construction of public works, which were of general interest, and which without such aid could not be carried out. The release from internal duties and tolls was found, however, to be the removal of so great an obstacle to Swiss prosperity that the Federal Assembly subsequently hesitated to permit the cantons to impose tolls for the support of public works, preferring instead to furnish pecuniary support directly from the federal treasury.

The articles of the constitution of 1848, involving the foregoing regulations, were brought under discussion in 1871, with a view to their revision, and the result of the discussion was a series of articles, which, with a single unimportant change, were adopted in the constitution of 1874. According to these articles, affairs concerning the customs duties belong to the Federation, which has the right to levy import and export duties. In levying these duties the following principles should be observed:—

1. Import duties should be as light as possible (*a*) on articles which are demanded for in-

ternal industry and agriculture; (*b*) on commodities required to satisfy the necessary wants of life; but articles of luxury should bear the highest tax. These principles should also be followed, if there are no opposing considerations, in forming commercial treaties with foreign powers.

2. Export duties should be made as light as possible.

3. The tariff legislation should embrace regulations calculated to secure the commerce of the frontier and the markets. The Federation retains always the right, under extraordinary circumstances, to adopt temporary special measures at variance with the above regulations.

The revenue derived from the customs duties belongs to the federal treasury. The sums previously paid to the cantons as compensation for their ancient duties, tolls, and other dues, are no longer paid. Exceptionally, however, the cantons Uri, Graubünden, Ticino, and Wallis, on account of their international Alpine roads, receive an annual subsidy, which has been fixed at the following figures: For Uri, 80,000 francs; for Graubünden, 200,000; for Ticino, 200,000; for Wallis, 50,000. Prior to the completion of the St. Gothard railway, the cantons Uri and Ticino together received also an annual subsidy of 40,000 francs for clearing the snow from the St. Gothard route,[1]

[1] Articles 28, 29, 30,

In setting aside internal duties certain taxes on consumption are allowed to stand, which, inasmuch as they were imposed chiefly on articles produced outside of the canton levying them, and were collected at the cantonal frontiers, appear as an exception under the law abolishing intercantonal duties. They were, moreover, treated as such an exception under Article 31, which guaranteed the freedom of commerce and industry throughout the Federation; and, in Article 32, the cantons were specifically authorized, in accordance with the provisions of the preceding article, to collect import duties on wine and other spirituous drinks, under the following limitations:—

1. In collecting these duties the transit shall be in no manner impeded, and the commerce in general shall be interfered with as little as possible and burdened with no other duties.

2. If objects imported for use are taken out of the canton, the duties that have been collected on them shall be returned without further burden.

3. Articles of Swiss production shall be subjected to duties lower than those imposed on foreign products.

4. The import duties on wine and other spirituous drinks of Swiss production, where such exist, shall not be increased, and they shall not

be introduced into cantons where they do not exist.

5. The laws and ordinances of the cantons regarding the collection of import duties, before they are carried out, shall be submitted to the federal authorities for approval, in order that the violation of existing principles may be prevented.

In Article 32 it was further provided that with the expiration of the year 1890, all import duties then being collected by the cantons, as also similar duties collected by individual communes, shall cease without compensation.

Among the obstacles to the common welfare were the privileges enjoyed by certain persons with respect to internal transportation. In many cantons exclusive privileges of transportation had been granted to certain corporations or communes. This was the case, for example, in the canton of Uri. Vessels belonging to Luzern might transport persons and wares to landing-places in Uri, but might not take away from these places either persons or goods, because Uri had given to a shipping company the exclusive right to do this. These monopolies produced serious commercial friction, which suggested federal interference; and the matter having been brought before the Diet, it was determined that free competition in the transportation of persons and goods, both by land and water, should be guaranteed to the citizens of all cantons. The essential principle of this resolution was embodied in the thirteenth article of the constitution of 1848. The federal legislature was given the right to make the necessary regulations concerning the abolition of existing privileges with respect to the transportation of persons and wares of every sort, between cantons or within any given canton.

The first legislative application of this constitutional provision was made in declaring the shipping free between Luzern, Flüelen, Brunnen, and Gerson. Before the revision of the constitution in 1874, all privileges with respect to transportation had been swept away, and thus the reason for the existence of Article 30 had disappeared. It was, therefore, not continued in the revised constitution, an adequate prohibition of privileges with respect to transportation being found in the constitutional provisions which guarantee freedom of intercourse and trade.

The federal government has not only broken down the hindrances presented by commercial privileges, and undertaken to guarantee freedom of intercourse and trade, but it has also been charged with the superintendence of the ways of communication. Although the construction of roads and bridges is primarily an affair of the cantons, yet, under the Act of Mediation, the Landamman of Switzerland might, in case of need, appoint inspectors commissioned to examine the routes, roads, and rivers. If work on these were urgently required, he might order it done; and, in case of necessity, he might cause to be executed directly, and at the expense of those to whom it belonged, such work as had not been begun or completed within the time prescribed.[1] The rights of the federal government to supervise the condition of the roads was, moreover, recognized in subsequent proposals for constitutional reform; and by the constitution of 1848 the Federation was authorized to exercise superintendence over the roads which it was interested in maintaining. According to Articles 26 and 33 of this constitution, certain sums were to be paid over to the cantons in compensation for customs duties and revenues from the post, which had been relinquished to the general government; but it was here provided that these sums might be retained by the Union, if the roads and bridges belonging to these cantons or corporations were not kept in the proper condition. At first, no permanent inspection was thought to be necessary, but since 1870 a bureau has been called into exist-

[1] Act of Mediation, Art. 23.

ence, at first under the postal department and later under the department of the interior, through which a permanent superintendence is maintained. The provisions of 1848 have been embodied in Article 37 of the present constitution, with only slight modifications. These modifications refer to the sums withheld by the Union, in case the roads and bridges are not kept in a proper condition.[1]

The Federation has, moreover, superseded the cantons in the control of postal affairs. Before 1848 these affairs were managed either by the several cantons directly or by other persons or bodies in contract with the cantons. The postal system was under direct cantonal management in Zurich, Bern, Luzern, Glarus, Freiburg, Solothurn, Basel-City, St. Gallen, Graubünden, Aargau, Ticino, Vaud, Wallis, Neufchâtel, and Geneva. In Uri it was farmed to the cantons Zurich and Luzern; in Basel-Land to Basel-City; in Schwyz to St Gallen; in Unterwalden to Zurich and Luzern; in Zug and Thurgau to Zurich; in Schaffhausen it was in the hands of

[1] The article of the present constitution in question is as follows: "La Confédération exerce la haute surveillance sur les routes et les ponts dont le maintien l'intéresse.

"Les sommes dues aux Cantons désignés à l'article 30, à raison de leurs routes alpestres internationales, seront retenues par l'autorité fédérale si ces routes ne sont pas convenablement entretenues par eux." Art. 37.

Prince Thun and Taxis. In the half-cantons of Appenzell communication was maintained without any regular postal arrangements.

Through the adoption of Article 33, of the constitution of 1848, an important step was taken towards unifying the postal service of Switzerland. The functions of the postal departments as they had existed in the cantons were transferred to the Federation. At the same time it was provided that the postal connections, which were maintained at the time of the transfer, should not be diminished without the consent of the cantons concerned; furthermore, that the rates of postage should be as low as possible and the same for the whole territory of the Federation; that the inviolability of postal secrets should be guaranteed; and that the Federation should offer compensation for the postal revenues relinquished by the several cantons. The conditions under which this compensation was to be rendered were as follows: 1. The cantons should receive annually sums equal to the average amounts of their net revenues from their postal systems for three years, 1844, 1845, and 1846. When, however, the net revenue collected by the Federation was less than the prescribed compensation, the deficit was borne by the several cantons in proportion to the compensation prescribed for each. 2. If a canton received from its postal system nothing directly, or, by reason of the terms under which it was farmed, much less than was actually collected by the person to whom it was farmed, such a condition of things should be taken account of in distributing the amounts of the compensation. 3. In case the postal system had been transferred to a private person or corporation, the Federation should undertake to compensate such person or corporation for relinquishing it. 4. The Federation was empowered and obliged to receive, at a fair compensation made to the owners, all material belonging to the postal system in so far as it was found to be serviceable. 5. The federal authorities were, moreover, empowered to rent or purchase the buildings then used in the postal service of the cantons.

On the first of January, 1849, the postal affairs of Switzerland passed under the authority of the Federal government. The arrangements at this time existing in the several cantons were provisionally adopted, and the whole system was placed under the authority of the Federal Council. During the same year the Federal Assembly passed laws embracing permanent postal regulations, which have become uniformly valid throughout the whole Federation. Under these laws provision is made for the transportation of letters, packages, and persons; for the organization of the postal administration; and for the determination of the rates of postage. By the law organizing the postal administration, the Swiss territory was divided into eleven districts, which took their names from the principal town in each. These are the districts of Geneva, Lausanne, Bern, Neufchâtel, Basel, Aarau, Luzern, Zurich, St. Gallen, Chur, and Bellinzona. At the head of the administration stands the Federal Council, which has the power to establish regulations and appoint officers. While to this body belongs the supreme control, it has delegated extensive powers to the Postal Department, which exercises supervision over the whole system, and has in turn delegated certain of its powers to subordinate officers. There is, then, a central directory, with general activity and supervision, and in each of the territorial subdivisions already named, a district directory. All officers are appointed for a term of three years, while the clerks hold for an indefinite period; but both may be removed at any time for cause.

In 1852 the Federal Assembly undertook to fix the amounts of the postal indemnity to be paid to the several cantons. The federal law on this subject left to each canton the privilege of seeking redress through the courts, in case of dissatisfaction with the amount fixed by the assembly. Under this privilege, only Neufchâtel and Basel-Land were successful in attempts to obtain an increase in the amounts prescribed, which in the case of the latter was followed by a corresponding reduction in the amount at first apportioned to Basel-City. The whole amount to be distributed was 1,486,560 francs and 94 centimes, of which the apportionment was as follows :—

Zurich was to receive............francs	232,138.46
Bern.................................. "	249,252.48
Luzern............................... "	57,958.18
Uri................................... "	29,771.10
Schwyz .... "	2,857.14
Unterwalden ob dem Wald........ "	342.86
Unterwalden nid dem Wald....... "	228.57
Glarus............................... "	10,329.83
Zug .... "	3,285.71
Freiburg............................. "	20,320.52
Solothurn............................ "	10,490.93
Basel-City .... "	119,065.25
Basel-Land.......................... "	16,758.61
Schaffhausen........................ "	3,181.82
Appenzell, Exterior................ "	14,285.71
Appenzell, Interior................ "	342.86
St. Gallen.......................... "	89,084.76
Graubünden........................ "	33,549.19
Aargau.............................. "	146,694.43
Thurgau............................. "	25,454.55
Ticino............................... "	14,908.96
Vaud .... "	207,812.91
Wallis............................... "	26,488.07
Neufchâtel.......................... "	74,676.33
Geneva.............................. "	97,281.71
Total..........francs	1,486,560.94

The rights of the Prince of Thun and Taxis in the postal affairs of Schaffhausen were purchased by the federal government for 150,000 francs. As compared with the total indemnity to be paid, the net postal income of the Federation under this order of things has sometimes shown a surplus, but oftener a deficit. In the revision of the constitution in 1874, the cantons agreed to forego their annual indemnity in view of a release from certain military burdens. Article 36 of the revised constitution, therefore, affirms that the postal and telegraphic systems throughout Switzerland belong to the federal government; that the revenue derived from them belongs to the federal treasury; that the rates should be as low as possible and the same for the whole territory of the Federation; and that the inviolability of postal and telegraphic secrets should be guaranteed.

For very good reasons the constitutional provision which was here established regarding the telegraph had had no place in the constitution of 1848. The law of December 23, 1851, however, placed it under the exclusive control of the federal government.[1] Whatever concessions were later made to private persons or corporations were issued by the Federal Council. These

[1] In France a decree of December 27, 1851, declared: "Aucune ligne télégraphique ne peut être établie ou employée à la transmission des correspondances que par le gouvernement ou avec son autorisation."

were made to persons or corporations for restricted use, chiefly to railway corporations, restricting the use of the telegraph to the service of operating railways. Since the passage, in 1852, of the general law regulating the construction and use of railways, a railway franchise carries with it the right to establish a telegraph line along the road to be used in conducting the business of the road. Funds for the direct construction of lines of telegraph by the federal government were received in 1852, as a loan, without interest, from private persons and cantons, for a period of five years. The lines at first established between the more important points were the beginnings of an elaborate system under direct federal management. The proposed plan to unite the postal and telegraphic systems under a single organization was finally set aside as tending to produce complications and friction rather than simplicity and facility of operation. The ends in view were found to be most surely served by giving to the telegraph the conditions of independent development, and bringing it into close co-operation with the postal department. Under the organization effected in 1854, the supreme administrative authority, as in the postal system, is vested in the Federal Council. Under the postal and telegraphic department, there is a central directory of telegraphic administration, and in each of six districts a subordinate directory. The officers are appointed either by the Federal Council or by other officers holding delegated authority from that body.

Before 1848 the several cantons held the right to coin money. Through the exercise of this right, through the lack of any central authority in this matter, and through the use of different foreign coins in different parts of Switzerland, the medium of exchange had become apparently hopelessly deteriorated. By the provisions of the constitution of this year, however, all rights of coinage were vested exclusively in the federal government. Power was, moreover, conferred on the federal government to fix regulations under which existing coins might be circulated or re-coined. Legislation under these provisions was had May 5, 1850. The franc, composed of one hundred *Rappen*, or *centimes*, was adopted; and the coins specified in the law, multiples or fractions of this unit, were made legal tender. In January, 1860, the federal legislature determined further details of the system here established; and, among others, the conditions under which French gold coins might circulate in Switzerland, what coins should continue to be struck as token money, and to what amount these token coins should be legal tender. Finally, in 1874, provisions essentially like those then in force were introduced into the revised constitution.[1]

The need of uniformity of weights and measures was recognized early in the movement towards national unity. In 1848 it was constitutionally provided that the union should introduce, on the basis of the existing confederate concordat, weights and measures which should be uniform throughout the Federation. Later the details of the system were determined by federal legislation. The power here exercised by the Federation was confirmed in that body by the fortieth article of the constitution of 1874; but the execution of the laws relating to these matters was left with the cantons, acting under the supervision of the federal authorities.[2]

All these provisions show a marked extension of the functions of the central government, which may be observed also in the recent legis-

[1] "La Confédération exerce tous les droits compris dans la régale des monnaies.

"Elle a seule le droit de battre monnaie.

"Elle fixe le système monétaire et peut édicter, s'il y a lieu, des prescriptions sur la tarification de monnaies étrangères." Art. 38.

[2] "La Confédération détermine le système des poids et mesures.

"Les cantons exécutent, sous la surveillance de la Confédération, les lois concernant cette matière." Art. 40.

lation regarding education. Surrounded by nations whose governments rested on monarchical traditions, and in which the instruction of youth was more or less colored by monarchical doctrines, it was important that such provisions should be made as would enable the youth of the republic to receive their education under influences favorable to the maintenance of the republican spirit. Moreover, in view of the antagonisms that existed between the German, French, and Italian cantons, and of the social friction that appeared between the adherents of the different creeds, it was important that the federal government should be in a position to strengthen and direct the forces which make for unity. Important among these forces are those which proceed from a wisely arranged system of public instruction. Down to 1848 all public schools had been in the hands of the cantons, but in the federal constitution adopted at that time, it was provided that the federal government might establish a university and a polytechnical school.[1]

At the first session of the federal legislature after the adoption of this constitution, a proposition to establish a university and a polytechnical school was presented and considered. A little later, in 1851, it was referred by the Fed-

[1] Constitution of 1848, Art. 22.

eral Council to a commission of ten experts from the different parts of the republic, who reported in favor of the project, but for various reasons, legislative action was deferred. In February, 1854, however, the proposition referring to a university having been rejected, a law was passed establishing a federal polytechnical school. The rejection of the university project did not indicate a determination to withdraw federal attention from the higher grades of academical instruction; for in the revised constitution of 1874 extensive powers were conferred upon the general government with respect to education. Under this constitution, the Union is empowered to establish, in addition to the already existing polytechnical school, a federal university and other institutions for higher education, or support such institutions. Under this provision, the federal legislature was left with the freedom of alternative action. It might, on the one hand, found an independent federal university and other institutions for higher instruction, or support those existing in the cantons; or, on the other hand, limit its activity to maintaining the polytechnical school.

The cantons provide adequate primary instruction, which must be placed exclusively under the direction of the civil authority. This does not mean that the clergy, if not Jesuits, shall be excluded from the positions of teachers and other school officers; if occupying these positions, they are required to stand on the same footing as laymen, and so to impart their instruction as not to do violence to the principle of freedom of conscience and belief. Although the primary schools are immediately under cantonal control, the cantons are not permitted to separate them into confessional schools; for it is required that the public schools must be so ordered and conducted that the adherents of all confessions may attend them without suffering in any manner with respect to their liberty of conscience or belief. Primary education is compulsory, and, in the public schools, free. Finally, the power to secure the proper observance of these provisions by the cantons is placed in the hands of the federal authorities, which " shall take the necessary measures against the cantons that do not comply with these obligations."[1]

"No penalties, however, were declared, and no means prescribed to force the cantonal government to carry the law into effect. Certain cantons not having fulfilled their duties in this respect, the Federal Assembly, in 1882, instructed the Federal Council to open an inquiry, and to take the necessary measures to insure general compliance with the constitutional law. In re-

[1] Swiss Federal Constitution. Art. 27.

ply the Federal Council proposed the creation of a Federal Department of Public Instruction, having under its orders a certain number of inspectors, whose duty it would be to see that the law was everywhere carried into effect. Agitation against this proposal at once began throughout the country, and in a short time a petition bearing upwards of 200,000 signatures, was forwarded to the central government. According to the Swiss constitution, if 30,000 citizens only demand a *plébiscitum*, any project voted by the Assembly must be submitted to the popular vote. In consequence, therefore, of so imposing a number of signatures, the Federal Council was obliged, much against its will, to submit the proposal to the popular vote, when it was rejected by 316,929 against 170,459 in its favor. To understand the real significance of this vote, it must be borne in mind that up to the present the Swiss cantons have enjoyed an almost absolute self-government, but that during the last few years the Federal Council has tried by every means to centralize power in its own hands. The cantons considered the proposed inspection to be a new attempt to deprive them of their autonomy, and therefore rejected it rather with a view to maintaining their rights than because they considered the project bad."[1]

[1] "Annual Register for 1882," p. 268.

In speaking of the relation of the schools to religion, Matthew Arnold says: "Whoever has seen the divisions caused in a so-called logical nation like the French by this principle of the neutrality of the popular school in matter of religion might expect difficulty here. None whatever has arisen. The Swiss communities, applying the principle for themselves and not leaving theorists and politicians to apply it for them, have done in the matter what they find suitable to their wants, and have in every popular school religious instruction in the religion of the majority, a Catholic instruction in Catholic cantons like Luzern, a Protestant in Protestant cantons like Zurich. There is no unfair dealing, no proselytizing, no complaint."[1]

Among the rights exercised for the common good by the federal government under the constitution of 1848, was the right, in the interest of the Federation or a great part of the same, to construct, or aid in the construction of, public works at the expense of the Federation. To this end, the Federation was authorized to exercise the right of eminent domain. The determination of details in this matter was left to federal legislation; and it was also competent for

[1] "Special Report on Certain Points connected with Elementary Education in Germany, Switzerland, and France." London, 1886, p. 8.

the Federal Assembly to prohibit the construction of public works which contravened the military interests of the Federation.[1] The construction and control of railroads were clearly within the scope of these provisions, and in December, 1849, this subject was brought to the attention of the Federal Assembly. In the spring of 1850, the Federal Council proposed a law regarding the exercise of the right of eminent domain, which was adopted by the Federal Assembly. This law had reference not merely to the construction of railroads, but also to the construction of any public works whatsoever, such as highways and improvements in water-courses, which the Federation might find it for its interest to further.

Under the provisions of the constitution, the federal legislature was free to make the construction and maintenance of railroads an affair of the state, or to leave their development to private enterprise. The latter course was chosen, as avoiding a degree of centralization which might be dangerous to the well-being of the Union. By a later federal law, concessions for the construction and use of railroads by private persons or corporations were to be sought immediately from the cantonal, but needed to be confirmed by the central, authority. Such con-

[1] Constitution of 1848, Art. 21.

firmation, however, could not be withheld except in cases where the construction of the road would violate the military interests of the Federation. The practical difficulties which arose through the exercise of these extensive powers by the cantons led the Federal Council to propose that the functions of the Union in railroad affairs should be materially extended and those of the cantons curtailed.[1] In keeping with this proposition was passed the federal law of December 23, 1872. By this law, the right to grant concessions to railroads, was vested solely in the hands of the federal authorities, yet the co-operation of the cantons was to be sought in the preliminary negotiations. "Through the railroad law of 1872," says Dr. Blumer, "the whole system of Swiss railroads was almost as completely centralized as the affairs of the customs duties, the post-office, and the mint."[2] The reason that little or no opposition was offered to this important movement toward greater centralization has been found in the lack of cantonal traditions regarding railroad affairs, and in the very evident need, in the limited territory of Switzerland, of unity of control.

The revised constitution of 1874 expressly sanctioned the condition into which railroad

[1] Blumer, II, 48.
[2] Blumer, II, 48.

affairs had been brought by previous legislation; for the constitutional provisions of 1848, regarding public works, were retained in the twenty-third article of the new constitution, and another article was added, the twenty-sixth, declaring that "legislation on the construction and management of railroads belongs to the Union." Under these provisions has grown up the elaborate railroad law of Switzerland.

Under the provisions of Article 23, the federal government has, moreover, contributed to the execution of other public works. Conspicuous among these are the works that have been constructed to confine the abundant waters of the country within their proper limits; such, for example, as the works on the upper Rhine and Rhone. But in controlling the water and forests of the mountains, the federal government acts under a special constitutional provision. This provision is contained in the twenty-fourth article of the present constitution, which confers upon the Union the right of supervision over the police charged with the immediate control of the forests and the works for the management of the water in the mountainous regions. The federal authorities contribute to the construction of these works, also to replanting the regions where the mountain streams have their sources. The federal authorities, moreover, take the measures necessary to maintain these works, and to preserve existing forests. Under these provisions, it is possible for the federal authorities either to take such positive and far-reaching action as would confine the cantons to mere police activity, or to make certain fundamental determinations and leave to the cantons a large and important sphere of operations. The latter course has been chosen.

Besides the rights here exercised with reference to material interests, certain other rights are conferred upon the Federation with reference to that class of the population known as the *Heimatlosen*, under which federal activity has been specially favorable to the social progress of the republic. Through various causes many persons had fallen into this class and become homeless; they had lost their rights of citizenship and residence, and, as vagabonds, were driven from canton to canton, and in their miserable wanderings sought shelter in barns and forests. By the existing constitution, it is ordered that the federal legislature shall take measures to give these persons a settled and recognized place among the inhabitants of the country, and to prevent new additions to this class.[1] In favor of social order is also the constitutional right which the federal authorities enjoy of ex-

[1] Article 68.

pelling from Swiss territory any foreigners whose presence endangers the internal or external security of the Union.[1] Switzerland offers an asylum to the members of all parties suffering political persecution, as long as they show themselves worthy of such consideration by peaceful conduct. The republic, however, grants them no asylum, if, while on its territory, they continue their intrigues and attacks on the existence and security of other states.[2] Although this hospitable policy has become customary, yet there are no grounds on which hospitality may be claimed by anyone under persecution.

The constitutional provision touching this matter is only negative in its indications; it confers the right to expel foreigners under certain conditions, but not the right to quarter them on any canton against the will of such canton.

However hospitable might be the designs of the Swiss with regard to persecuted foreigners, yet, as compared with the United States, their rugged country presents few resources through which refugees may find daily support or a betterment of their fortunes. In fact, the meager resources of Switzerland have made it annually necessary for a certain part of the native population to emigrate. Between the end of 1868 and

[1] Article 70.
[2] Blumer, II, 252.

the end of 1877, 35,158 persons emigrated from twenty cantons and half-cantons, exclusive of Uri, Frieburg, Solothurn, Vaud, and Geneva. These facts seemed to indicate that some general control of emigration and the agents through which it was furthered, was desirable. The constitution of 1848 contained no provision regarding this subject; it was, however, taken up by the federal legislature, and later recognized in the thirty-fourth article of the existing fundamental law.

In determining what the federal government may do towards increasing the common prosperity, the Swiss have not seen fit to leave the Federal Assembly and the Federal Tribunal any great discretionary power. Through the constitution they have determined specifically many things which under a general provision might have been clearly interpreted to belong, as the case might be, to either federal or cantonal authority. Of such articles of specific authorization, many have already been considered. In this list may also be placed Article 69, which empowers the Union to pass laws regarding sanitary police regulations concerning cattle pests and such epidemics as threaten the public health; Article 34, which confers upon the Federation the right to legislate with respect to the employment of children in factories, the hours of work for adults, and the means of protecting laborers against such employments as endanger their health or safety; and Article 35, which gives the federal authorities the right to take the necessary measures with respect to lotteries, and in which at the same time it is directly declared that the erection of gambling houses is prohibited, that those in existence must be closed on the 31st of December, 1877, and that all concessions granted or renewed after 1871 were null and void. In the same class belongs, moreover, Article 25, which authorizes the federal government to establish regulations under which hunting and fishing may be carried on, with the view of preserving the larger game, and also such birds as are useful to agriculture and forestry.

The most important act, comprehensive of many others, towards the attainment of the common prosperity of the several lands now united under federal control was the transfer of sovereignty from the individual cantons to the Union. The internal revolution which is marked by this transfer of power, and whose constitutional results are set forth in the preceding pages, introduces a new period in the history of Swiss institutions. The cantons as individual organisms do not stand as isolated facts in the political history of Europe. They are representatives of a large class of political organizations which became conspicuous in the later centuries of the middle ages. The fact that has given them special significance is their union and the development among them of social and political ties which have established the essential conditions of national life and growth. This revolution, effected by the peaceful processes of constitutional amendment and legislation, has placed the events of Swiss history during the last fifty years in line with the movements towards unity which have been carried on in Italy and Germany, and by binding the several cantons so firmly under a central power as to remove the liability of disintegration, has justified the emphasis here given to the establishment of federal institutions as the most important achievement in the political history of Switzerland.

INDEX.

Aargau, 32, 36, 37, 41, 45, 52.
Act of Mediation, 34, 36, 39, 43, 46, 47, 48, 95, 168, 189, 190, 203, 221
Alliances, early, 20; not permitted to cantons without consent of Diet, 25; with France, 33, 42, 189; of cantons, 168, 171; for const. guarantees, 52.
Allies, 43; invade Swiss territory, 43; determine integrity of S., 44; accord neutrality, 45, 46.
Ambassadors, received by Diet, 24; by cantons, 25; in the Diet, 48.
Amendment, of Swiss Const., 57; of U. S. Const., 58; of Mexican, 59.
Appenzell 5, 19, 20, 32, 45, 54, 63.
Arbitration, court of, in S., 154, 156.
Argentine Republic, 56; const. preamble, 57; const. amended, 60; distribution of power in, 93; ratio of rep., 98; suffrage, 99.
Aristocracy, in England, 64, 78; origin of, 80; in Greece, Italy, Netherlands, Switzerland, 81.
Articles of union, 1291, 15, 16.
Association, right of, 217.
Austria 17, 21, 22, 37, 45.
Basel, 19, 40, 45; division of 5.
Belief, freedom of, 213.
Bern, joins the union, 1353, 17; her policy, 17; quota, 28; divided, 32; territory taken from, 36; lands to Vaud., 37, 40, 41; seeks pre-revolutionary conditions, 43, 45, 49, 52, 157.
Bishoprics, 214.
British N. Am. Act, 89, 100, 147.
Burgermeister of *Vorort*, 49.
Cantons, primitive purposes of, 11; increased, 13-19, 36; sovereignty of, 29; new, 1798, 32; in military affairs, 193; comp. with States, 181.
Cantonal consts. revised, 50; 178.
Capital punishment, 220.
Capitulations, military, 176.
Catholic cantons, 6; defeated, 54.
Catholics and Protestants, union, 7.
Censorship, 216.
Centralization demanded in military affairs, 27; need of, in S., 28, 35; of 1798, effect of, 38; 69, 241.

Centralists, 33-35.
Citizens, representation of, 98.
Citizenship, 207-212; loss of, 210.
Civil rights, 210.
Children, 215; employment, 52.
Class distinctions in S., 8.
Coinage, 240.
Congress of Vienna, Swiss ambassadors at, 45; neutrality, 46, 86.
Conscience, rights of, 6, 213.
Constitution, violation of, 223; of 1798, a step towards centralization, 32; 29-32; of 1815, 44-54, 46; of 1848, opposing cantons, 5; 54-55; of U. S., makers of, 6; revision of, 167.
Consts. guranteed, 38, 47, 166, 223.
Courts, 1798, 31; of the U. S., 140; jurisdiction of, 150-152; of the Argentine Republic, 141; Canadian, relation to English and U. S., 146-151; in S., 153-163.
Convents, 214.
Customs duties, 194, 195, 227, 228.
Defensional, 28.
Democracy, in conflict with feudalism, 11; French, 29; return to 63.
Diet, 23; meetings of, 23; summoning the, 24; powers of, 24; subordinate States represented in, 24; only organ of the Conf., 23, 26; under Act of Mediation, 41; powers of, 41; at Zurich sets aside the Act of Mediation, 43; of 19 cantons at Zurich, 1814, 44; cantonal rep. in, 48.
Directorial canton, 40, 42.
Directory, 1798, 31-33.
Distribution of power, 56-96.
Divorce, 215.
Duties, by cantons, 227, 229, 230.
Education, 242.
Emigration, 251.
Empire, Swiss lands in relation to, 10.
Equality, 3, 4; of States, 108, 203,
Executive, 121-139; in Canada, 122; in Germany, 123; in Am., federal republics, 125; in U. S., 125; Mexico, 127; Col. 128; S, 133.
Exemptions from military tax, 198.
Extradition, 172-186.

(255)

INDEX.

Federal Assembly, elects Federal Tribunal, 156; determines seat of Fed. Trib., 157; decides questions of jurisdiction, 159, 169, 179; convoked, 180.
Federal Council, in Germany, 106; members of, 109; officers of, 134; salary of, 135; powers of, 135; relation to legislature, 135; distribution of functions, 137; compared with English Cabinet, 138; 169; in foreign affairs, 172; on foreign service, 175; 179; informed of internal conflicts, 180.
Federal tribunal, after 1874, 157; salaries, 157; place of meeting determined, 157, 169, 179.
Foreigners, 251.
France, 21, 22; alliance with, 25; crisis in, 33; enlists Swiss, 42, 45, 85.
Free trade between cantons, 221.
Freemen, assembly of, 18.
Freiburg, 18, 19, 37, 40.
Glarus, 17, 32, 45.
Graubünden, 1, 7, 37, 41, 228.
Gurantee of constitutions, 51 52, 165.
Gunpowder, 195, 197.
Helvetic Republic, 20, 29, 30, 33, 189.
Independence, 19, 20, 21.
Initiative, 116.
Instruction, primary, 243.
Intolerance, religious, 212.
Jesuits, 53, 214, 243.
Judgments, civil, 179, 187.
Judiciary, the, 140-163.
Jurisdiction of federal courts, 150-153; of Swiss Federal Tribunal, 158-162.
Landamman, 40, 42, 49, 232.
Liquors, revenue from, 195.
Luzern, 14, 16, 17, 28, 40, 49, 52, 157.
Majority rule, 26.
Marshall, Chief Justice, 164.
Marriage, 214, 215.
Mercenany service, 172-175.
Monopolies in transportation, 230.
Napoleon, points out need of S., 34; withdrawal of the army, 35; deals with the new cantons, 37-42.
Neufchâtel, 45, 54, 167.
Nobility, title of, 177.
Pardon, 162.
Parties, city and country, 17, 18.
Pensions, foreign, 176.
Post and telegraph, 194.
Power, distribution of, 56-96; re-distribution in England, 74; source of, 80; drift of in Germany, 86; *expressly* delegated, 93-96.
President, of legislative bodies, 111; election by minority, 129; election in Argentine Republic, 129; in Colombia, 129; qualifications, 130; election in Mexico, 130; term 131; case of vacancy, 132; conditions of re-election, 133; in S., 134.
Press, freedom of, 215, 217.
Privileges in transportation, 230.
Public works, 41, 246, 249.
Railroads, 247-249; tax on, 201.
Referendum, 117-120.
Relations, foreign, 164; internal, 178.
Representatives, 65, 81, 83, 104.
Revenue, 194.
Rights, political, 48, 223, 203-205.
St. Gallen, 24, 28, 32, 36, 37, 41, 45.
St. Gothard, 2, 228.
Salaries of legislators, 112, 113.
Sanitary regulations, 252.
Sarnen, league of, 52.
Schaffhausen, 1, 2, 19.
Schwyz, 5, 13, 45, 52.
Secession, 43; of 1846, 53.
Secretary, 42; general, 50.
Senate, 1798, 30; in federations, 105.
Senators, 106, 108, 112.
Settlement, right of, 207.
Shipping, 231.
Solothurn, 18, 19, 40, 52.
Sonderbund, 52.
Speaker, 111-112.
Spirit Monopoly Bill, 196.
Sovereign, 57, 60, 61.
Sovereignty, 29, 30, 46, 47, 253.
Stantz, agreement at, 18.
Suffrage, conditions of, 99, 208.
Supreme Court, 74, 140, 141, 145, 149.
Switzerland, critical period, 19; territory, 1; as ally, 21; as independent State, 21; aristocracies in, 81.
Tariff system, 226; tax, military, 197.
Telegraph, 238-240.
Territorial changes, 20, 164, 165.
Territory guaranteed, 165.
Thurgau, 5, 37, 52.
Ticino, 1, 2, 7, 37, 45, 228.
Titles, foreign, 176, 177.
Tolls for public works, 227.
Treaty power, 171.
Troops, 26, 40, 42.
Unterwalden, 5, 13, 45, 52.
Uri, 5, 13, 45, 52, 63, 228, 230.
Vaud, 36, 37, 41, 45.
Vorort, 24, 49.
Wallis, 5, 45, 52, 228.
Weights and measures, 241.
Worship, right of, 212, 213.
Zug, 5, 17, 32, 45.
Zurich, 14, 17, 28, 40, 41, 43, 49, 52.

www.ingramcontent.com/pod-product-compliance
Lightning Source LLC
Chambersburg PA
CBHW021346230426

43666CB00006B/421